Cooking for One Is Fun

Cooking for One Is Fun

HENRY LEWIS CREEL

Foreword by Craig Claiborne

Times
BOOKS

Illustrations by Lethe Black

Library of Congress Cataloging in Publication Data

Creel, Henry Lewis.
    Cooking for one is fun

    Includes index.
    1. Cookery. I. Title.
TX652.C78   1976   641.5'61   75-37370
ISBN 0-8129-0632-2

20 19 18 17 16 15 14 13 12 11 10

Contents

Foreword

The name of the author of this book is apt to be familiar to anyone who has paid close scrutiny to my cookbooks during the past couple of decades. *The Chinese Cookbook*, which I wrote with Virginia Lee, is dedicated "To Henry Creel, who washed all those woks." In a book on cooking with herbs and spices, a veal and pepper loaf is attributed to him. And in *The New York Times Cook Book*, the first book of all, his name (I just discovered to my astonishment) can be found five times in the index. It appears as "Creel's pepper hash, Henry," "Green pepper(s) hash, Henry Creel's," "Henry Creel's pepper hash," "Peppers hash, Henry Creel's," and "Pepper, Henry Creel's."

Several years ago, in fact, while visiting my local supermarket in East Hampton, I bumped shopping carts with an acquaintance who is in the publishing field.

"John," I said, "meet Henry Creel."

"How do you DO," he said, pumping Henry's hand with enthusiasm. "So nice to meet Mr. Pepper Hash himself."

Henry and I have been friends for more years than I really like to total, and many's the time I've dined on the specialties of his kitchen in his neatly furnished apartment in Manhattan; agreeable meals, indeed, for he is an excellent cook and as he goes about his preparations the kitchen remains admirably spotless. Mr. Clean, himself.

For many years Henry worked as an accountant for the Shell Oil Company in New York. In 1969 the company moved their headquarters to Houston, and Creel, then approaching retirement age, decided to take an early retirement. He is an inveterate movie- and theater-goer, and wild horses could not have wrenched him away from that metropolis—New York—which he adores.

Although Henry has always liked to putter about the kitchen, I think his real "in-depth" interest—his thoroughgoing indoctrination—in cookery actually came about when I built a house in East Hampton.

In pursuit of my job with *The New York Times,* I have cooked in that kitchen, with rare exception, every weekend alongside my great good friend and colleague, Pierre Franey, former chef of Le Pavillon Restaurant and one of the most distinguished chefs in America. During those sessions—Henry doing the dirty work with the pots and pans at the sink—the author of this book has kibbitzed with considerable enthusiasm. After those cooking sessions, started some 15 years ago, Henry would report each week that he had re-created one dish or another for his own pleasure in his apartment in the city. It wasn't so surprising to learn that he had made a small beef stew for one, cooked a lamb chop in some sauce, or even made a single helping of flan. What did boggle the mind was the day he announced that he had mastered the technique of making *crêpes* for one! Crêpes, incidentally, are one of his breakfast favorites. He makes two cornmeal crêpes, which are lightly buttered and eaten with bacon, perhaps, or breakfast sausages. Then he cooks two more crêpes which he dines on with jam or marmalade.

There is a small, decidedly ill-kept assortment of apple trees outside my kitchen window which, each year, produce an enormous harvest of gnarled, mottled, pockmarked fruit. One year Henry took back with him on the 3:06 to Manhattan a small batch of these apples in his suitcase. When he got home that night he turned them into a small batch of applesauce. For one. Another year he gathered a quart or less of beach plums from the bushes that surround my mail box. These I generally let shrivel on the branch. Henry took them home and made about half a cup of beach plum jelly.

If you are familiar with the food columns of *The New York Times*—I share a byline with Pierre on Sundays—you may find some vague resemblance to recipes you've noted before. We have given Henry our blessings in altering anything he chose for the man or woman who lives and cooks alone.

Henry loves to cook. And I share with him the theory that for those who love it, there is no greater therapy. Feel sorry for yourself because you live alone and prepare your own meals? Ridiculous. It's easy and fun as you're apt to discover in perusing this book.

CRAIG CLAIBORNE

Introduction

Like most bachelors and others who live alone by accident or by choice I started cooking for two reasons. I'm not sure which one takes precedence. One reason was necessity: I simply couldn't afford to eat in the kind of restaurant that prepares food well and serves it with style. Two, I like to cook. Like many another cook, I think it is the greatest therapy known to man or woman. What could be more rewarding than cooking for an appreciative audience—even if it is an audience of one.

Since leaving my family hearth many years ago—about forty to be exact—I have always prepared my own food, but it was not until I retired from my gainful employment in 1969 that I really turned to cooking with a passion. I had been active for a number of years as an accountant for a major oil firm and when the company moved its headquarters from New York to Houston I was given a choice of moving or staying. I opted to stay in Manhattan for I was comfortably settled in a nice modest-sized apartment on the East Side, with a nice, modest-sized kitchen, no larger and not much more elaborately equipped than thousands of other kitchens in the city.

For many years I have spent weekends in East Hampton watching (and washing dishes) in the kitchen of a couple of friends of long standing—Craig Claiborne and Pierre Franey. I have sampled a few thousand meals that came from their stove. On returning from these visits, I have frequently, with their good wishes—and a knowing smile or two—adapted their thoughts to cooking for one person. I have also adapted a few hundred of my family recipes into portions adequate for the solo diner.

Today, I cook almost every meal for myself, except on weekends when I visit friends. With rare exceptions I cook with simplicity and without a lot of tedious folderol. The side effects are rewarding: I have the pleasure of creation. I feel at home in my bachelor quarters with those fine odors coming from the kitchen. I control my weight by preparing just enough to give my stomach and my taste buds pleasure. And there is also an economic gain in cooking precisely the amount to meet my pleasure and needs.

This collection of recipes dates from a little after retirement when I bought a typewriter and learned to type. It was my habit to enter the ingredients in a note book in the kitchen and to guess at reasonable quantities to make a serving for one. When luck or trial-and-error led to a dish that pleased me, I typed the recipe from my notes and filed it for future use. In five years or so I had a collection of over 300 recipes I could reuse and recommend.

My ideas for recipes came from various sources: from memories of dishes from my childhood in Jefferson City, Missouri; from eating experiences at home and abroad; from reading many current publications on the subject.

It is obvious that cooking small portions presents the problem of buying in small quantities or of preserving quantities purchased but not required for the recipe. I have, of course, purchased the exact quantities required from my market on occasion; however, I enjoy shopping in the convenient and less expensive supermarket. There I have found a package problem, but one not insurmountable. The answer is preservation of unrequired quantities by refrigeration, freezing, or cooking. I purchase a whole chicken and cut it into parts and freeze the parts not immediately needed. Since I prefer white meat chicken, I often buy one breast of chicken or the smallest number packaged. Since half a breast is generally enough for one serving, I wrap the remainder in wax paper and place it in the freezer for later use; or in the refrigerator if it will be used the next day. Sometimes I poach the other half of a chicken breast and use it in chicken salad, in chicken à la king, or in some other dish in which cooked chicken is required. Cooked chicken can be stored for several days in the refrigerator.

So far as ground beef is concerned I frequently buy the smallest portion that I can find in the supermarket which usually comes to about a pound and this I cut into four portions and press into patties. A quarter of a pound is usually enough for one serving in dishes that include other ingredients. The other three portions of the pound of ground beef are wrapped in wax paper and frozen for future use. Of course, for a single hamburger I often use slightly larger portions of meat. Ground beef can be wrapped in waxed paper and stored in the refrigerator for several days.

Dividing and conserving also applies to other food items. In cooking for one it is important to pay attention to purchasing smaller packages of ingredients and conserving portions not required for the recipe at hand. Careful consideration in buying and storage is most rewarding in this day of rising food prices. I always cook with fresh ingredients, seldom with packaged frozen foods or canned foods except for chicken and beef broth, gravy, tomatoes, and such. However stews, chili, and combinations improve with a little aging. Leftovers I have kept to a minimum and discarded, purposely forgetting orders from my youth to eat everything on my plate. I have found health and a more comfortable belt in this manner of eating and that is why buying and cooking to size is to be recommended.

I sincerely hope these recipes will satisfy your appetite as they have mine and that you will find pleasure in your kitchen—alone or with limited company. I mean by that last remark that these recipes for one can easily be doubled or tripled and used as building blocks for a larger meal. But take caution and test the seasonings and watch the cooking times.

Cooking for One Is Fun

Soup

Asparagus Soup • Asparagus and Onion Soup
Boston Bean and Stewed Tomato Soup • Navy Bean Soup
Meal-in-Itself Soup • Scotch Broth
The Quickest Borsch • Cabbage Soup
Soup de Chou • Chicken Noodle Soup with Tomatoes
Chicken-Leek Soup • Clam Chowder • Cream of Carrot Soup
Cream of Celery Soup • Cream of Corn Soup
Corn Chowder • Gazpacho
Leek and Potato Soup • Vichyssoise • Onion Soup Gratinée
Potato-Onion Soup • Puree of Fresh Vegetable Soup with Cheese
Tomato Soup • Tomato Puree Soup

What a good dish for lunch—either by itself or accompanied by a salad or sandwich. Soup is equally welcome at the start of any meal. And what a good way to make something to enjoy out of leftover vegetables, sauces, meats, and juices.

There is infinite latitude in composing a soup. One knows this from the variety of soups available in commercial establishments: from lightly disguised water to rich double consommé, from thick cream soups to hearty vegetable conglomerates. These variations are easily controlled by the ingredients and the cooking times. The richer soups, of course, are more expensive to prepare and more likely to be higher in calories. Remember this if you are not trying to put on weight. Some of the less rich soups, made with milk instead of cream, are very good and satisfying. The decision on richness is yours—you can always elect to switch to heavy cream and additional butter in any of the recipes that follow. If you do, you must be prepared to accept the consequences in terms of calories and carbohydrates.

My favorite is a light cream soup using a pureed vegetable in a sauce of flour and milk. The basic plan is to boil a vegetable in little water and seasonings to the tender stage; puree the vegetable by using a food mill, sieve and spoon, blender or ricer, or whatever you have and prefer; reduce the remaining liquid by boiling rapidly until it is almost consumed and add to the puree; melt butter and stir in flour to form a thickening element for the milk which is whisked in and stirred until it begins to thicken; join and mix well the sauce and the puree and serve hot. You can try it with almost any vegetable. You can even skip the pureeing, but this process makes a smoother, more enjoyable, and certainly more elegant soup.

ASPARAGUS SOUP

2 tablespoons margarine or butter
½ medium onion, chopped
4 large stalks asparagus, peeled and sliced
½ cup water
2 cups milk
2 teaspoons salt
Freshly ground black pepper
2 new potatoes, boiled and sliced

1. Heat 1 tablespoon margarine or butter in a saucepan and sauté the onion until translucent.
2. Add the asparagus and water and simmer 15 minutes.
3. Reduce the liquid to about 1 tablespoon by rapid boiling.
4. Add milk, seasonings, potatoes, and remaining butter. Bring to the boiling point and serve.

ASPARAGUS AND ONION SOUP

6 asparagus tips, in 1-inch pieces
1 onion, thinly sliced
Salt and pepper
½ cup milk
1 tablespoon butter

1. Put the asparagus and onion in a saucepan and add water to cover. Add salt and pepper and simmer ½ hour or until the vegetables are tender.
2. If there is too much liquid remaining, remove vegetables and reduce to 1 tablespoon by boiling rapidly for a few minutes.
3. Return vegetables to the pan, add the milk and butter, bring to a boil, and serve in a hot dish.

BOSTON BEAN AND
STEWED TOMATO SOUP

1 8- to 9-ounce can Boston baked
   beans

1 8- to 9-ounce can stewed
   tomatoes
1 cup water

Place all ingredients in a saucepan and simmer for ½ hour.

Note: You may want to add salt and freshly ground pepper.

NAVY BEAN SOUP

¼ cup navy (pea) beans
¼ cup diced country ham or salt
   pork
1 small onion, chopped
   Salt and pepper
3 cups water

1 rib celery, diced (optional)
2 shakes crushed red pepper
   (optional)
1 teaspoon flour
2 tablespoons water

1. Wash the dry beans well and place in a saucepan with all ingredients except the last two.
2. Simmer at least 2 hours. You may prefer the beans cooked a little more to tender.
3. Shake the flour and water in a small jar with a top to blend or stir well in a cup or glass. Add to the soup and stir well until it is thickened.
4. Serve with one tablespoon green tomato relish or India relish or tomato ketchup.

MEAL-IN-ITSELF SOUP

8 ounces beef shank
1 onion, sliced
1 8-ounce can stewed tomatoes
1 teaspoon salt
1 stalk of celery, cut in 1-inch pieces

1 small leek, split and cut in 1-inch pieces
1 carrot, sliced

Place all ingredients in a vessel, cover tightly and simmer 2 hours or longer. Test for seasoning, adding pepper if desired, and serve hot.

SCOTCH BROTH
(Lamb and Barley Soup)

1 small lamb shank trimmed of fat and excess tissue
1 teaspoon butter
  Salt and pepper
1 small onion, chopped
1 garlic clove, minced
2 small turnips, diced

1 carrot, diced
2 cups water
1 medium tomato, peeled, cored, and diced
2 tablespoons pearl barley
2 tablespoons split peas

1. In a saucepan, melt the butter and brown the lamb for about 5 minutes, stirring.
2. Add salt and pepper, onion, and garlic. Stir and cook another few minutes.
3. Add the water, bring to a boil and simmer 45 minutes.
4. Add the turnips, carrot, and tomato and simmer another 30 minutes. Remove the lamb and let cool.
5. Add the barley and peas and simmer for 40 minutes longer until the barley and peas are tender.
6. Bone the lamb and discard the bones. Cut the lamb meat into bite-size pieces and add to the soup. Serve hot.

THE QUICKEST BORSCH
(Mock)

1 8¼-ounce can sliced beets and juice (approximately 1 cup)

2 cups Sherry-Kraut (see recipe, page 216)

Combine ingredients and simmer 20 minutes.

Note: Makes several servings of a filling, nonfattening lunch. If you prefer a thin soup, add a cup or so of beef stock, if available, or an equal amount of canned beef broth.

CABBAGE SOUP

2 tablespoons butter
1 tablespoon chopped onion
½ cup shredded cabbage

1 tablespoon flour
1 cup milk, warmed

1. Melt half the butter in a saucepan and sauté the onion until it changes color. Add the cabbage and cook until the cabbage is tender.
2. In another saucepan melt the remaining butter and stir in the flour. When well blended, add the milk and stir until the roux begins to thicken.
3. Put the cabbage and onion through a food mill or strainer and add to the sauce. Serve hot.

SOUP DE CHOU
(French Cabbage Soup)

1 cup diced cabbage
1 cup chicken broth
1 tablespoon diced onion

Salt and freshly ground black pepper

1. Simmer all ingredients in a saucepan until the onion and cabbage are tender.
2. Puree the vegetables in a blender or food mill.
3. Check the soup for seasonings, and serve hot.

CHICKEN NOODLE SOUP WITH TOMATOES

⅔ cup concentrated broth (see note)

2 tablespoons elbow or other macaroni

⅓ cup tomatoes, strained
Salt and pepper

⅓ cup milk

1. Place all ingredients except milk in a saucepan, bring to a boil, and simmer 15 minutes or until the macaroni reaches your preferred tenderness.
2. Stir in the milk and serve immediately.

Note: To obtain ⅔ cup concentrated broth, reduce contents of an 8-ounce can of broth by boiling.

CHICKEN-LEEK SOUP
(Inspired by Cock-a-leekie)

½ chicken breast with ribs and wing or your favorite pieces of chicken

3 small leeks, in 1-inch slices

1 13¾-ounce can chicken broth or water
Salt and pepper

4 prunes (optional)

1. Place the chicken in a pot with cover. Add the well-washed slices of 1 leek and the broth.
2. Bring the pot to a boil and simmer covered about 2 hours or until the chicken is well done. Remove the chicken and let cool.

3. Clear excessive grease on the top of the pot by absorbing in several paper towels.
4. Add the remaining leeks, and salt and pepper.
5. Simmer covered to tender adding the prunes (if desired) in the last 5 minutes.
6. Bone the cooled chicken and add to the soup. Serve hot.

Note: Rice may be added, if desired, in the last 20 minutes or so of cooking time. Use about 2 tablespoons of uncooked rice. Test for desired doneness before serving.

CLAM CHOWDER

2 tablespoons diced ham, salt pork, or bacon	1 small potato, diced
	Salt and pepper
1 onion, chopped very fine	1 cup milk
4 ounces minced clams and juice	

1. Fry the ham or pork in a saucepan. Add the onion and cook, stirring until the onion begins to turn translucent. Add the clams and juice and bring to a boil.
2. Add the potato, salt and pepper and cook until the potato is tender.
3. Add the milk, bring to a boil, and serve hot.

Note: Cream instead of milk and a pat of butter added on top at the last moment make this a more delicious chowder, but beware the calories.

CREAM OF CARROT SOUP

1 small white onion, sliced	1 cup milk
2 carrots, sliced	1 teaspoon salt
1 tablespoon butter	Freshly ground black pepper
1 tablespoon flour	

1. Simmer the onion and carrots in water to cover until tender.
2. Puree through a sieve or food mill.
3. In a saucepan melt the butter, then blend in the flour. When well blended add the milk, stirring rapidly.
4. When the roux is smooth and thickened, add it to the pureed vegetables and mix well.
5. Season with salt and pepper and serve hot.

CREAM OF CELERY SOUP

3 ribs celery, finely diced	1 tablespoon flour
1 medium onion, sliced	1 tablespoon butter
Salt and pepper	1 cup milk
1 teaspoon sugar	Parsley (optional)

1. Place the celery and onion in a saucepan with salt and pepper and sugar, cover with water and boil rather rapidly until the celery is tender (about 15 minutes).
2. Puree by passing through a food mill or potato ricer, or blend in a blender for a few seconds.
3. In another saucepan melt the butter, then stir in the flour. When well mixed pour in all the milk at once, stirring with a wire whisk. Continue stirring until the sauce begins to thicken.
4. Add the pureed vegetables to the sauce, mix well with the whisk, garnish with parsley and serve hot.

Note: Butter may be added to the soup just before serving to improve the taste. Cream or half-and-half may be substituted for milk if you can stand the calories. The soup is also good without the sauce and its butter; just stir the milk into the puree, garnish and serve.

CREAM OF CORN SOUP

1 ear cooked corn (see page 200), cut from the cob
1 cup milk
2 teaspoons butter
2 teaspoons flour
Salt and pepper
2 drops worcestershire sauce

1. Place the corn in a blender with a dash of the milk and blend 3 seconds.
2. Melt the butter in a saucepan and stir in the flour. Cook 1 minute and add the remaining milk, stirring vigorously with a wire whisk.
3. Cook stirring until the roux begins to thicken.
4. Add the corn, salt and pepper. Serve hot, stirring in the worcestershire sauce at the last minute.

CORN CHOWDER

1 teaspoon vegetable oil or butter
1 medium onion, chopped
2 tablespoons chopped green pepper
2 ears cooked corn, cut from the cob
1½ cups milk
Salt and freshly ground pepper

1. Heat the oil in a saucepan and sauté the onion and green pepper until wilted, about 3 minutes, stirring constantly.
2. Add the corn and stir. Continue cooking another minute or so.
3. Add the milk and salt and pepper. Mix well and bring to a boil. Simmer about 10 minutes and serve hot.

GAZPACHO

1 teaspoon olive oil	1 medium tomato, coarsely
½ garlic clove, minced	chopped
¼ cup chopped onion	½ cup chopped cucumber
2 tablespoons chopped green	2 tablespoons wine vinegar
pepper	⅔ cup tomato juice
	Salt and pepper

1. In a saucepan, sauté the garlic in the oil for 1 minute and add the other vegetables. Stir and cook 1 minute longer.
2. Place in a blender and blend for about 5 seconds.
3. Add the vinegar, tomato juice, salt and pepper and blend another 5 seconds.
4. Refrigerate until thoroughly chilled. Serve cold with garnishes and bread sticks.

Note: Garnishes are optional but interesting as well as more elegant. In Madrid, chopped tomatoes, chopped cucumber, chopped green pepper, and toasted bread cubes or croutons are common garnishes.

LEEK AND POTATO SOUP

1 tablespoon butter, melted	⅓ cup chopped onions
1 medium leek, chopped	1 cup chicken broth
⅓ cup chopped potatoes	Salt and freshly ground pepper

1. Cook the vegetables in the butter, stirring frequently for about 5 minutes.
2. Add the chicken broth and continue cooking until the potatoes are tender, about 15 minutes longer.
3. Season to taste with salt, add pepper and serve hot.

Note: This plain soup may be made with water instead of chicken broth, which makes it less rich and pleasing to the taste. It is richer, more delicious and even elegant with the addition of 2 tablespoons of heavy cream.

VICHYSSOISE

Blend the Leek and Potato Soup or pass it through a food mill or sieve. Return the pureed soup to the pan and heat to boiling. Add 2 tablespoons of heavy cream and serve hot or chill and serve cold. Chopped chives can be sprinkled on top before serving.

ONION SOUP GRATINEE

1 tablespoon butter
1 garlic clove, minced or put through a garlic press
1 onion, thinly sliced (½ to ⅔ cup)
  Salt and freshly ground pepper
1 teaspoon flour

1 cup water (beef or chicken broth, if you like it richer)
  A pinch of thyme
¼ bay leaf
½ slice toast
1 tablespoon or more grated cheese (Gruyère or Parmesan)

1. Melt the butter in a saucepan and sauté the garlic for a minute or so. Add the onion and continue cooking over low heat until the onion wilts, stirring constantly.
2. Add salt and pepper, stir and cook for a minute.
3. Stir in the flour and mix well.
4. Add the water or other liquid, thyme, and bay leaf; cover and simmer for 30 minutes.
5. Cut the toast in half and place on top of the soup in an oven-proof small casserole or soup bowl (individual earthenware bowls are recommended). Sprinkle with cheese and place under the broiler (at about 350 degrees) until the cheese has melted and the soup is bubbling.

POTATO-ONION SOUP

1 tablespoon butter	½ cup chicken broth
½ cup diced onion	½ cup milk
½ cup diced potatoes	Salt and pepper

1. Cook onion in the butter in a saucepan, stirring, for several minutes.
2. Add potatoes and broth and bring to a boil.
3. Simmer until the potatoes are tender (about 25 minutes).
4. Puree the vegetables through a food mill and keep warm.
5. When ready to serve, stir in the milk and bring just to a boil. Season.

Note: This soup will be richer in taste and calories with half-and-half or cream.

PUREE OF FRESH VEGETABLE SOUP
WITH CHEESE

1 carrot	½ cup water
1 onion	½ cup milk
1 potato	2 tablespoons grated Parmesan
1 celery rib	cheese (optional)
1 tomato	

1. Slice all the vegetables thinly so that they will cook quickly.
2. Place in a saucepan over medium heat, add water and simmer 45 minutes, partially covered. You can use a sheet of aluminum foil over the pan to hold in heat.
3. Pass the vegetables through a food mill to puree.
4. Return the puree to the cooking pan and stir in the milk. Check seasoning and serve with a sprinkling of cheese.

Note: Cream or half-and-half instead of milk will taste richer and contain more calories. If you are not afraid of calories, top this soup with a pat of butter just before serving.

TOMATO SOUP

2 ripe tomatoes, cored, peeled
   and diced
2 tablespoons chopped onion
¼ teaspoon celery seed
1 garlic clove, minced

½ bay leaf
2 tablespoons butter
2 tablespoons flour
2 cups milk
   Salt and pepper

1. Place tomatoes in a saucepan and add onion, celery seed, garlic and bay leaf. Simmer until tomatoes are soft.
2. In another saucepan, melt the butter and add flour stirring over low heat to blend.
3. Bring the milk to a boil and add to the flour and butter mixture, stirring constantly.
4. Strain the tomatoes into the sauce when it begins to thicken. When well blended, add salt and pepper and serve.

TOMATO PUREE SOUP

1 tablespoon butter
1 tablespoon flour
1 cup milk
⅓ cup tomato puree

½ teaspoon salt
   Pepper (optional)
3 drops worcestershire sauce

1. Melt the butter in a saucepan and blend in the flour. Cook for 1 minute.
2. Add the milk all at once while stirring vigorously. Continue stirring until the mixture begins to thicken. It thickens more quickly over higher heat, but lower heat and more time ensure success.
3. Add remaining ingredients, mix well and bring to a boil. Check seasonings and serve hot.

Beef

Home-Style Roast Beef • Pan-Broiled Filet Mignon
Fillet of Beef with Port Wine
Steak with Shallots and Wine Vinegar • Pepper Steak
Shell Steak with Madiera-Brandy Sauce
Barbecued Round Steak
Chicken-Fried Round Steak with Cream Gravy
Round Steak with Green Pepper • Sauerbraten
Rare Roast Beef with High Heat • Pot Roast with Vegetables
Simmered Beef Brisket • Pot Roast Without Liquid
Beef Pot Pie • Quick Beef Stew • Saffron Beef
French Beef Stew • Beef Stew with Beer and White Onions
Hungarian Goulash-1 • Hungarian Goulash-2
Hungarian Goulash-3 • Beef Casserole • Beef and Tomatoes
Beef, Tomatoes, and Green Pepper • Beef Stew with Wine
Beef à la Provençale • Beef Daube Provençale
St. Patrick Stew • Home-Style Hash • Braised Short Ribs
Boiled Beef • Pot au Feu-1 • Pot au Feu-2
Cooked Beef Sauté with Onions and Potatoes
Individual Meat Loaf-1 • Individual Meat Loaf-2
Individual Meat Loaf-3 • Individual Meat Loaf with Carrots
Ground Beef and Mashed Potato Loaf • Beef-Ham Loaf
Fruity Meat Loaf • Hamburger • Frenchburger
Hamburger au Poivre • Ground Meat Patty with Cream Sauce
Meatballs-1 • Meatballs-2 • Spanish Meatballs
Meatballs Stroganoff • Beef Curry • Curried Beef with Peas
Stir-Fried Ground Beef and Vegetables
Ground Beef, Celery, and Tomatoes • Ground Beef and Peppers
Ground Beef and Stewed Tomatoes • Beef Picadillo
Picadillo • Ground Beef with Dill • Chili

Chili with Tomato Paste • Potato and Chili Casserole
Chili Mac • Chili, Tex-Mex Variety • Hot Tamale Pie
Scalloped Potatoes and Hamburger • Macaroni-Beef Medley
Eggplant and Beef Casserole • Ground Meat Casserole
Zucchini-Beef Casserole • Stuffed Zucchini
Ground Beef Stew Without Water • Ground Beef Stew

In my hometown, restaurants offered very good country ham, other pork products, chicken, turkey, and quail, but I ordered T-bone steak when my parents occasionally took me out to dinner. It is an ordering habit I have held onto in later years. I trust restaurants to prepare steak and roast beef fairly well; it's not that difficult. Just how good it will be depends mostly on the quality of the meat.

I have often prepared steak and roast beef and I recommend pan-fried filet mignon or steak (pages 23 and 25) for a quick and easy meat course. My favorite roast beef recipe (page 29) is for rare roast beef cooked briefly in a very hot oven and allowed to rest in the closed oven for about an hour after the heat has been turned off. I like to cook sirloin tip or another tender cut of beef by this method, but if you have received a tough piece of beef that is difficult to masticate with pleasure, there are ways to incorporate any leftover portion in recipes that use small cubes of cooked beef.

In cooking for myself over the years, I have had the greatest pleasure in creating recipes that surprise and delight the palate using ground beef or cubed beef as the main ingredient. That is why I have chosen to include quite a few recipes for meat loaf, chili, meatballs, goulash, hash, curry, and various casseroles. In these and similar preparations I have felt the thrill of creation and I have enjoyed the flexibility afforded.

Don't be afraid to appease or develop your particular taste by adjusting seasonings, cooking times, and even by adding a favorite herb. The pleasures of creating and adjusting to suit are enormous.

21

HOME-STYLE ROAST BEEF

⅓ pound roasting beef (freeze the remainder of the smallest market package for another dish)
Salt and freshly ground pepper

1 teaspoon flour
1 teaspoon vegetable oil
1 small onion, cut in half
1 small carrot, sliced
¼ cup water

1. Dredge the beef in a mixture of salt, pepper, and flour. Reserve the seasoned flour.
2. Heat the oil in an ovenproof casserole and brown the beef on all sides.
3. Add the onion, carrot, and water.
4. Cook the beef in the oven at 350 degrees for 1 hour or until tender. Remove from the casserole.
5. With a fork, mash the onion and carrot into the juices in the casserole. Shake the reserved flour with a small amount of water in a small jar with a lid. Over a low flame, stir in the flour and continue stirring until slightly thickened.
6. Pour the sauce over the beef and serve.

PAN-BROILED FILET MIGNON

½ pound fillet of beef
1 teaspoon salt

1 teaspoon butter
Parsley

1. Wipe the meat with a damp cloth or paper towel and trim any excess fat.
2. Heat a small frying pan over a moderate flame and sprinkle the bottom with salt.
3. Place the beef in the center of the pan and cook for three minutes, moving the meat in the salt to prevent burning and sticking.
4. Turn the meat and continue cooking for another three minutes, moving the meat as before so that it will not stick to the pan.

5. Remove the meat to a warm plate and top it with a teaspoon of butter and parsley. Serve immediately.

Note: Cooking time varies according to taste and thickness of the meat. This recipe will make a rare, 1-inch fillet. Other cuts of steak can be treated similarly with good results.

FILLET OF BEEF WITH PORT WINE

2	teaspoons butter	1	tablespoon beef gravy
6	ounces fillet of beef	2	tablespoons port wine
1	or 2 sliced mushrooms	3	drops lemon juice
1	tablespoon chopped onion		Salt and pepper

1. Melt 1 teaspoon of butter in a skillet and brown the beef on both sides. Set aside.
2. In the other teaspoon of butter cook the sliced mushrooms for about three minutes, stirring constantly.
3. Add the onion and continue cooking and stirring for another minute.
4. Add the beef gravy, port wine and lemon juice. Blend well and set aside until serving time.
5. In an iron skillet or other ovenproof vessel, bake the beef at 350 degrees for 20 minutes. Let the beef rest out of the oven for several minutes.
6. Remove the beef to a warm plate and add the sauce to the baking vessel after pouring off accumulated fat. Stir the sauce, dissolving any brown particles that cling to the bottom of the vessel. Boil and reduce the sauce to desired thickness and serve with the fillet.

STEAK WITH SHALLOTS AND WINE VINEGAR

⅓ or ½ pound filet mignon (you may use other cuts, but fillets come in small pieces and if they are too thick, can be sliced in two and used for another day or another dish)

1 tablespoon butter
Salt and pepper
1 tablespoon shallots, finely chopped
2 tablespoons red wine vinegar
¼ teaspoon chopped parsley

1. Trim excess fat from the fillet.
2. Melt the butter in a frying pan, salt and pepper the steak, and cook 3 minutes on each side for rare or longer as you like it.
3. Remove the steak to a warm serving plate and add the shallots to the frying pan.
4. Cook the shallots, stirring constantly, for 1 minute and stir in the wine vinegar.
5. When the liquid is reduced to 1 tablespoon, pour over the steak and serve with parsley garnish.

PEPPER STEAK
(Steak au Poivre)

⅓ pound filet mignon or sirloin (or ½ pound, according to your appetite)
2 teaspoons peppercorns
Salt

1 tablespoon butter
1 tablespoon finely chopped shallots
1 tablespoon cognac
¼ teaspoon chopped parsley

1. Trim any excess fat from the steak.
2. Crush the peppercorns well with a mortar and pestle.
3. Rub the crushed pepper into the steak on both sides and press in with your hands. Salt to taste.
4. Melt the butter in a skillet and cook the steak on both sides

to desired doneness (3 minutes on each side for rare) over medium heat.

5. Remove the steak to a warm serving plate. Add the shallots to the skillet, stir quickly, and pour in the cognac. Stir again and pour over the steak. Serve hot with a sprinkling of parsley.

SHELL STEAK WITH MADIERA-BRANDY SAUCE

1 steak
1 teaspoon oil
  Salt and pepper

1 tablespoon madiera wine
1 tablespoon brandy

1. Heat the oil in a small skillet and sear the steak on both sides.
2. Salt and pepper the steak and cook over moderate heat for 4 minutes on one side and 3 minutes on the other, pouring off any accumulation of oil or fat when turning.
3. Remove steak to a warm plate, pouring off all fat from the frying pan.
4. Turn off the fire, return pan to the stove and add wine and brandy. Stir to dissolve any brown particles in the skillet, and pour sauce over the meat. Adjust seasoning.

BARBECUED ROUND STEAK

1 small round steak, 5 to 8 ounces (½ pound)
1 tablespoon flour
  Salt and pepper
2 teaspoons vegetable oil
½ cup minced onion
½ cup green pepper, sliced

1 small garlic clove, minced
½ cup canned tomatoes
2 teaspoons brown sugar
2 teaspoons worcestershire sauce
2 teaspoons lemon juice
½ teaspoon prepared mustard
1 shake Tabasco

1. Pound a mixture of the flour, salt and pepper into the beef.

2. Brown the beef on both sides in the oil.
3. Remove the beef to a small casserole. Sauté the onion, green pepper, and garlic in the oil remaining, adding more if required. Add to the casserole.
4. Combine the tomatoes, brown sugar, worcestershire sauce, lemon juice, mustard and Tabasco. Pour over the beef.
5. Bake covered at 350 degrees for 1½ hours.

CHICKEN-FRIED ROUND STEAK WITH CREAM GRAVY

1 egg	4 ounces round steak, cut in
¼ cup milk	1-inch strips
2 tablespoons flour	2 tablespoons heavy cream
Salt and pepper	1 tablespoon vegetable oil

1. Mix the egg and milk together well. Mix the flour with the salt and pepper. Dip the meat in the liquid and then in the flour; coating well.
2. Fry at very low heat in the oil, turning to cook both sides, for about 20 minutes.
3. Remove the meat and set aside, keeping it warm. Add the cream, stirring all the residue from the pan into the sauce. Serve the cream sauce over the meat.

ROUND STEAK WITH GREEN PEPPER

5 to 6 ounces round steak	2 tablespoons chopped onion
Salt and pepper	½ garlic clove, chopped
1 tablespoon butter	½ teaspoon worcestershire sauce
½ cup tomato sauce	½ cup chopped green pepper

1. Salt and pepper the steak on both sides.
2. Melt the butter in a skillet and brown the steak well on both sides, over moderately high heat.
3. Add the remaining ingredients and simmer over low heat for 1 hour, turning the steak after ½ hour.
4. Reduce the sauce in the pan after removing the steak by turning up the fire and stirring. When it thickens, pour over the steak on a warm platter and serve.

SAUERBRATEN

½ pound bottom round or similar cut roast beef (see note)
Salt and freshly ground pepper
¼ cup wine vinegar
¼ cup water
1 garlic clove, minced
3 peppercorns

¼ cup sliced onion
1 bay leaf
1 tablespoon sugar
1 clove
1 tablespoon tomato paste
Flour for dredging
1 slice bacon

1. Season the meat with salt and pepper and place in a small bowl or casserole with cover (you can improvise a cover with aluminum foil).
2. In a saucepan, make a marinade of the vinegar, water, garlic, peppercorns, onion, bay leaf, sugar, clove, and tomato paste, bringing to a boil.
3. Pour the marinade over the meat, cover and refrigerate overnight. Turn the meat over in the marinade once, the next morning.
4. About 3 hours before eating time, remove the meat from the marinade, dry thoroughly with paper towels, and coat on all sides with flour.
5. Dice the bacon and fry it in a small casserole. Brown the meat well on all sides in this grease.
6. Add the marinade and bake covered for 2½ hours at 350 degrees.
7. Serve slices of the sauerbraten with the remaining marinade

sauce. This may need some thickening with a water and flour mixture.

Note: In the supermarket or wherever meat is packaged, you may find it convenient to purchase two pounds of roast or more. If so, cut into several pieces and freeze part for another day or another dish.

RARE ROAST BEEF WITH HIGH HEAT

1 pound sirloin or other tender cut of beef

1 tablespoon flour
Salt and freshly ground pepper

1. Heat the oven to 500 degrees or as high as it will go.
2. Flour, salt and pepper the beef, rubbing the flour in well.
3. Place the beef in an open roasting pan in the oven.
4. Roast 5 minutes and shut off the heat; do not open the oven door. Leave the roast inside the oven for at least 1 hour. It is now ready to serve but can easily be held for another cocktail, up to another hour. Leave the oven door closed until serving time.

Suggestion: Serve the roast with pan gravy which may be extended by the addition of a little water. Test the seasoning or have salt handy at the table. Save any leftovers; they will be good cold or can be used in recipes calling for cooked beef.

POT ROAST WITH VEGETABLES

Salt and pepper
½ pound brisket of beef
1 tablespoon olive or vegetable oil
1 garlic clove, minced
1 onion, chopped

1 tablespoon tomato paste
1 teaspoon worcestershire sauce
2 tablespoons water
1 carrot, sliced
1 leek, well washed and sliced

1. Salt and pepper the roast. Oil a skillet and brown the roast on all sides over medium-high heat. Remove the meat and keep it warm.
2. Add to the skillet the garlic, onion, tomato paste, worcestershire sauce, and approximately one tablespoon of water and cook over medium heat for 1 or 2 minutes, stirring constantly.
3. In a suitable casserole with a cover, make a bed of the carrot and leek. Place the roast on the bed of vegetables.
4. Pour the skillet seasonings over the meat in the casserole, rinsing the skillet with a tablespoon or so of water.
5. Cover and bake in a 350 degree oven for 1½ hours.
6. Remove the meat from the casserole and puree the vegetables by pressing them through a sieve or food mill. Retain the liquid which pours off first in the pureeing process. Place this liquid in the freezer or the refrigerator until a crust of grease has formed and can be skimmed and discarded (it's fattening if you don't discard the grease).
7. Return the pureed vegetables to the casserole, place the meat on top and add the skimmed liquid. Cover and keep warm until serving time. Serve the meat with the puree as a sauce.

SIMMERED BEEF BRISKET

8 to 10 ounces brisket of beef
1 medium onion, sliced
1 garlic clove, cut in three pieces
2 or 3 carrots, quartered
2 cloves
1 bay leaf

Salt
5 peppercorns
2 small leeks, washed, trimmed, and sliced
2 small potatoes, peeled

1. Place the beef in an ovenproof casserole with cover; add water to cover and bring to a boil over medium heat. Simmer 30 minutes, skimming the scum from the top as necessary.
2. Add the rest of the ingredients except the potatoes, cover again, and simmer another 30 to 45 minutes.
3. Add the potatoes and simmer covered for 1 hour.
4. Remove the vegetables and meat and reduce the liquid by rapid boiling or thicken with 1 teaspoon of flour shaken well with 2 tablespoons of water in a small jar with top. If you like more richness, use a blend of 1 teaspoon of flour and 1 of butter to thicken the sauce. Add this gradually to liquid stirring constantly.
5. Replace the meat and vegetables, cover, and keep warm until serving time.
6. Slice the meat to serve and pour the sauce over it. You can also serve the overcooked vegetables, although they are less elegant.

Note: Two tablespoons of prepared horseradish at serving time makes a most delightful additive to the sauce. Mix well and serve over the meat.

POT ROAST WITHOUT LIQUID

½ cup chopped onion
1 garlic clove, minced

7 to 8 ounces brisket of beef
Salt and freshly ground pepper

1. Place the onion and garlic in a small casserole with a tight-fitting cover and top with the brisket which has been salted and peppered on both sides.
2. Cook covered over low heat on top of the stove, using a flame tamer, or covered in the oven at 300 degrees, for 3 or 4 hours.
3. Reduce the liquid, if any, by boiling rapidly, and serve over the brisket.

Note: If desired, you may brown the brisket a bit more under the broiler.

BEEF POT PIE

1 tablespoon vegetable oil
6 ounces beef chuck or any stew beef, in small cubes
1 garlic clove, minced
2 tablespoons chopped onion
Salt and pepper
1 teaspoon flour
2 carrots, in one-inch slices

4 mushrooms, sliced
1 tablespoon tomato paste
½ teaspoon thyme
1 bay leaf
½ cup water
Pastry crust (see recipe, page 224)

1. Brown the meat in the oil in a skillet at high heat, stirring constantly.
2. Add the garlic, onion, salt and pepper, stir and cook another minute.
3. Sprinkle with flour and stir well.
4. Add the other ingredients and simmer ½ hour or until meat is tender.

5. Pour the stew into a small ovenproof vessel and cover with pastry crust. Bake ½ hour at 400 degrees. Let rest 5 minutes before serving. Brown the crust on top by putting it in the broiler a few minutes and serve hot and steaming.

QUICK BEEF STEW

¾ pound stewing beef, in 1-inch cubes
Flour for dredging
1 tablespoon vegetable oil
1 carrot, sliced

2 sprigs parsley
1 garlic clove, minced
1 medium onion, sliced
1 cup sherry
Salt and pepper

1. Dredge the beef in flour and brown it in the oil in a skillet over medium high heat.
2. Place the browned beef, carrot, parsley, garlic, onion, sherry, salt and pepper in a casserole. Simmer covered for 1 hour. Use a flame tamer or a very low flame, and stir occasionally.
3. Remove the beef and vegetables to a warm serving plate.
4. Prepare the remaining liquid in the casserole as a sauce to serve over the beef and vegetables. Reduce and thicken the liquid by boiling rapidly or add a mixture of flour and water, well blended, and stir into the sauce.

SAFFRON BEEF

1 tablespoon vegetable oil or butter
1 medium onion, sliced
1 small garlic clove, minced
Salt and pepper
7½ ounces brisket of beef or bottom round

½ small green pepper, cubed
½ medium tomato (3½ ounces), cored, peeled and cubed
¼ teaspoon thyme
¼ teaspoon saffron
4 ounces tomato sauce

1. Preheat the oven to 325 degrees.
2. Heat the oil or butter in a casserole with a tight-fitting cover. Add the onion and garlic, salt and pepper and cook until the onion is wilted but not browned.
3. Add remaining ingredients and bring to a boil. Cook covered in the oven for 1½ hours or until the meat is tender.

Suggestion: Serve with rice.

FRENCH BEEF STEW
(Inspired by Boeuf en Daube)

6	to 8 ounces beef shank or chuck or any inexpensive cut, in cubes	2	sprigs parsley
	Salt and pepper	¼	teaspoon rosemary
1	cup dry red wine	2	slices bacon, cut in small pieces
2	tablespoons chopped onion	1	tablespoon flour
1	garlic clove, minced	3	cherry tomatoes
1	carrot, sliced	1	shallot
½	bay leaf	1	teaspoon butter
¼	teaspoon thyme	4	stuffed olives

1. Marinate the beef for 5 or 6 hours in the wine seasoned with salt, pepper, onion, garlic, carrot, bay leaf, thyme, parsley, and rosemary.
2. Preheat the oven to 350 degrees.
3. Cook the bacon in a small casserole until it is crisp. Remove and reserve.
4. Drain the beef and add to the casserole in which the bacon was cooked. Cook, stirring, for 5 minutes.
5. Remove the vegetables from the marinade and set it aside. Add vegetables to the meat and cook for 5 minutes longer.
6. Sprinkle in the flour and stir to coat the meat on all sides.
7. Bake uncovered for 10 minutes.
8. Add the marinade and cook uncovered for another hour.
9. Remove the beef and pass the sauce and vegetables through

a food mill or potato ricer. Add the meat to the pureed sauce and keep warm.

10. Blanch the tomatoes in boiling water and peel them. Chop the shallot and sauté it 1 or 2 minutes in the butter.
11. Cook the olives a minute in boiling water and add with tomatoes, bacon, and shallot to the stew. Serve hot.

BEEF STEW WITH BEER AND WHITE ONIONS

2 slices lean bacon, diced	1 teaspoon flour
½ teaspoon butter	Salt and pepper
3 small white onions, peeled	2 ounces beer or enough to cover
½ garlic clove, minced	the meat
⅓ pound boneless round or chuck steak in cubes	½ teaspoon lemon juice

1. Pour boiling water over the bacon and let it stand 2 minutes. Drain.
2. In the butter fry the bacon until translucent.
3. Add the onions and garlic and cook until golden. Place in a casserole, leaving the butter in the skillet.
4. Brown the beef in the butter and add it to the casserole.
5. Stir in the flour, salt and pepper. Add beer to cover the meat.
6. Bring to a boil, then turn down heat and simmer on top of the stove for 1½ hours. Use a flame tamer and stir occasionally to prevent scorching.
7. Right before serving time, stir in the lemon juice.

Note: If the sauce is too thin, boil it at high heat and reduce to desired consistency. Serve with noodles or rice or French or Italian bread.

HUNGARIAN GOULASH—1

1 tablespoon flour
¼ teaspoon salt
¼ teaspoon pepper
½ teaspoon paprika

1 cup lean club or round steak, cubed
1 tablespoon butter
¼ cup tomato puree
¼ cup beef gravy

1. Mix flour, salt, pepper and paprika and coat the meat evenly on all sides.
2. Heat the butter in a frying pan or small casserole and brown the meat quickly on all sides.
3. Add the tomato puree and beef gravy, cover and bake at 300 degrees for 1 hour.

Note: This dish may be prepared in advance and warmed just before serving.

HUNGARIAN GOULASH—2

1 tablespoon oil
⅔ cup onions, coarsely chopped
5 ounces beef roast, cut in ½-inch cubes

2 tablespoons tomato paste
2 tablespoons paprika
Salt

1. Heat the oil in a casserole or pan with cover and cook the onions until golden brown.
2. Add the beef and stir until its red color becomes grayish.
3. Add the tomato paste, paprika, and salt. Cover and simmer 2 hours.

HUNGARIAN GOULASH—3

¼ pound beef chuck steak, in
½-inch cubes
1 tablespoon flour
¼ teaspoon salt
1 teaspoon vegetable oil
1 teaspoon paprika
1 teaspoon cider vinegar

¼ teaspoon caraway seeds
¼ teaspoon marjoram
½ teaspoon chopped capers
¼ bay leaf
2 sprigs of parsley, minced
2 tablespoons dry sherry
1 tablespoon tomato paste

1. Dredge the beef cubes in a mixture of the flour and salt.
2. Brown the beef in the oil in a skillet.
3. Add the remaining ingredients, mix well, and simmer covered for ½ hour. Keep warm until serving time.

BEEF CASSEROLE

¼ pound beef, cubed
1 teaspoon bacon drippings
1 small onion, sliced
1 carrot, sliced

½ cup yellow turnip, diced
1 celery rib, diced
Salt and freshly ground pepper
1 tablespoon barley

1. Preheat the oven to 350 degrees.
2. Brown the cubes of beef in the bacon drippings.
3. Add all the other ingredients and cover with boiling water.
4. Bake covered for 1 hour and remove from the heat.
5. Serve hot in a warm bowl.

BEEF AND TOMATOES

½ cup finely chopped onion
2 teaspoons oil
¼ pound beef, in small cubes
(about ¾ cup)
¾ cup quartered cherry tomatoes
or diced tomatoes

1 tablespoon water
¼ teaspoon cornstarch
2 tablespoons sherry
Salt and pepper

1. Sauté the onion in one teaspoon of the oil for 4 minutes over medium low heat, stirring constantly.
2. Add the cubed beef and continue stirring for several minutes until the beef changes color and is cooked to medium rare (about 4 minutes). Keep warm.
3. Heat the remaining teaspoon of oil in a skillet and add the tomatoes. Stir and cook over low heat for 3 minutes.
4. Blend the water and cornstarch (by shaking together in a small jar) and stir the mixture into the tomatoes.
5. Combine the meat and tomatoes. Mix well and stir in the sherry just before serving. Add salt and pepper. Serve on a heated plate.

BEEF, TOMATOES, AND GREEN PEPPER

1 teaspoon oil
¼ cup minced onion
¼ cup chopped green pepper
3 ounces beef, in small cubes
(approximately ½ cup)

5 cherry tomatoes, quartered, or
2 ripe tomatoes, diced
¼ teaspoon cornstarch
1 tablespoon water
2 tablespoons sherry
Salt and pepper

1. Heat the oil in a skillet. Sauté the onion and green pepper for 3 minutes over medium high heat, stirring constantly.
2. Add the beef and continue cooking and stirring until the meat changes color (about 3 minutes).

3. Add the tomatoes and cook, stirring, another 3 minutes.
4. Mix the cornstarch and water well (shaking in a small jar) and stir the mixture into the meat and vegetables.
5. Stir in the sherry just before serving. Add salt and pepper to taste.

BEEF STEW WITH WINE

½ pound beef in ¼-inch cubes (round steak is good for this)
Flour for dredging
2 tablespoons vegetable oil
Salt and freshly ground pepper
1 garlic clove, minced
2 carrots, finely chopped
2 small leeks, coarsely chopped
2 tablespoons chopped parsley
2 onions, sliced
1 bay leaf
¼ teaspoon thyme
¾ cup dry red wine

1. Dredge the meat in flour and brown well in the oil over high heat.
2. Add the other ingredients and cook until the vegetables are brown, stirring occasionally.
3. Pour the wine over the meat and vegetables, bring to a boil, cover and simmer for 2 hours.

Optional:

2 small white onions
2 small mushrooms
1 tablespoon butter
1 tablespoon flour

1. Add the white onions and the mushrooms ½ hour before the stew is done.
2. Stir the butter and flour together into a paste and add to the stew a little at a time. Stir until the desired thickness is obtained.
3. Serve with rice or noodles. A small leftover portion will be good for a lunch tomorrow or anytime in the next week.

BEEF A LA PROVENCALE

1 tablespoon flour
Salt and freshly ground pepper
½ pound boneless chuck steak, cubed
2 teaspoons olive oil
2 teaspoons butter
2 tablespoons chopped onion or one small onion, chopped
1 garlic clove, minced

¼ cup dry red wine
1 tablespoon tomato paste
1 celery rib, cut in two
½ bay leaf
1 sprig parsley
½ teaspoon thyme
Beef broth
6 green olives, pitted

1. Dredge the meat in a flour, salt, and pepper mixture, coating all sides. Brown well in the oil and butter in a skillet, over rather high heat. Transfer the meat to a heavy casserole.
2. Add the onions and garlic to the oil in the skillet. Cook until golden. Add to the casserole. Pour the wine into the skillet and stir to dislodge any brown particles. Add the tomato paste, stir, and cook 1 minute.
3. Pour the liquid over the meat, add the celery, bay leaf, parsley, and thyme, and add enough broth to moisten the stew (about ½ inch).
4. Cover and simmer for 2 hours, or until the meat is tender.
5. Remove the celery and add the olives after simmering them 2 minutes in boiling water.

Note: Small quantities of carrots and potatoes may be added as a vegetable in the last hour or so.

BEEF DAUBE PROVENCALE

6 ounces beef chuck or plate, cubed
1 garlic clove, sliced
1 carrot, sliced

1 small onion, sliced
½ bay leaf
¼ teaspoon thyme
¼ teaspoon parsley

¼ teaspoon rosemary
½ cup red wine
   Salt and freshly ground pepper
1 slice bacon or salt pork, cubed

1 tablespoon flour
4 pitted green olives
4 cherry tomatoes, peeled, or 1 medium fresh tomato, diced

1. Marinate the beef in the garlic, carrot, onion, bay leaf, thyme, parsley, rosemary, wine, salt and pepper for at least 8 hours or overnight.
2. Preheat the oven to 350 degrees.
3. In a casserole cook the bacon until crisp and set it aside.
4. Drain the beef and reserve the marinade and vegetables.
5. Add the cubes of beef to the casserole and cook, stirring, for 5 minutes. Add the vegetables. Cook, stirring, another 5 minutes.
6. Sprinkle with flour and stir to coat the beef.
7. Bake uncovered 20 minutes.
8. Add the marinade and enough water to just cover the beef. Bring to a boil on top of the stove, then cook covered in the oven for 1½ hours.
9. Remove the beef from the casserole and strain the vegetables, pressing them to release all juices.
10. Return the beef vegetables and juices to the casserole and add the olives, tomato, and bacon. Warm and serve.

ST. PATRICK STEW

3 tablespoons flour
1 teaspoon paprika
   Salt and pepper
1½ pounds stewing beef, in 1-inch cubes
3 tablespoons vegetable oil
2 medium onions, sliced

1 garlic clove, finely minced
2 carrots, coarsely sliced
1 turnip, coarsely sliced
2 small potatoes, coarsely sliced
¼ teaspoon thyme
1 bay leaf
1 teaspoon sugar

1. Combine flour, paprika, salt and pepper on a sheet of wax paper and coat beef. Set aside remaining flour mixture.

2. Brown coated beef well in the oil and remove from the skillet.
3. Add onions and garlic to the skillet and cook for two minutes.
4. Add browned beef and cover with water; top with the vegetables and the seasonings.
5. Simmer for 2 hours, removing the potatoes, carrots, and turnips as they become almost tender to the feel of a fork. Do not overcook vegetables. Thicken the liquid with the remaining flour mixture, shaken together with a small amount of water.
6. At serving time replace the vegetables, bring stew to a boil, and simmer for 5 minutes.

Note: This will feed one person 2 or 3 times. The stew keeps well and can be varied by accompanying starches, such as biscuits, rice, pasta.

HOME-STYLE HASH

2 tablespoons vegetable oil	2 small new potatoes, diced
1 onion, diced	Salt and freshly ground pepper
¼ pound round steak, cubed	3 tablespoons water
1 tablespoon flour	

1. Heat the oil in a small casserole and sauté the onion for 5 minutes, stirring constantly.
2. Add the steak and cook uncovered until the meat loses its red color. Stir to distribute the meat over the hot surface. Sprinkle the meat with flour and stir again.
3. Add the potatoes, salt, pepper, and water. Cover the casserole and simmer 1 hour. Use a flame tamer and low heat. Without the flame tamer, stir more frequently.
4. Thicken the sauce, if desired, with a flour and water mixture. Use 1 teaspoon of water and 1 of flour shaken together in a jar.

BRAISED SHORT RIBS

1 pound short ribs of beef	½ cup onion, diced
Salt and pepper	¼ teaspoon thyme
½ cup carrots, diced	1 bay leaf
½ cup celery, diced	

1. Tie rib or ribs together with string so they will not fall apart in cooking. Salt and pepper them and place in a casserole. Bake uncovered at 350 degrees for 1½ hours.
2. Remove the meat from the casserole and pour off any accumulated fat.
3. Add to the casserole the vegetables, thyme, and bay leaf. Stir to mix well.
4. Place the short ribs on the vegetables and seasonings, cover, and return to the oven for 1½ hours.
5. Untie the ribs and serve with the vegetable mixture.

BOILED BEEF

1 tablespoon oil	1 onion, chopped
½ pound beef, brisket, round or chuck	1 leek, finely chopped
	1 carrot, chopped
1 garlic clove, minced	Salt and pepper
	½ cup water or beef broth

1. Heat the oil in a skillet, brown the meat on all sides, and remove it to a casserole with a heavy lid.
2. Add the garlic and onion to the skillet. Cook until golden, stirring occasionally, and add to the meat in the casserole.
3. Add the leek and carrot to the casserole with salt and pepper to taste.
4. Pour water or beef broth over the meat, cover, and simmer 2 hours or until the beef is quite tender.
5. Remove the meat from the casserole. Puree the vegetables by

putting them through a food mill and place in a saucepan with any cooking liquid remaining. Reduce the puree over high heat to about ½ cup. Serve the sauce over the meat while hot.

POT AU FEU—1
(Simple French Beef Stew)

9	ounces beef (brisket is good)	2	cloves
2	white onions, quartered	½	bay leaf
1	garlic clove, minced	3	peppercorns
1	carrot, sliced		Salt
1	leek, split, well rinsed and tied with string	½	medium zucchini, trimmed and cut in ½-inch slices
		1	medium potato, quartered

1. Place the beef in a kettle, cover with water and bring to a boil. Simmer the beef over low heat for about 5 minutes, skimming the foam from the top.
2. Add the other ingredients except the zucchini and potato and simmer covered for 1 hour.
3. This stew may be prepared in advance. About an hour before serving time, add the zucchini and potato and simmer until the potato is tender and the beef is well done.

Note: Serve with horseradish or tomato or mustard sauce. The remaining liquid is good as it is as soup, or it may be used as the base for another soup.

POT AU FEU—2

½ pound beef shank or other cut
of beef
1 onion, sliced
½ cup canned tomatoes
1 carrot, sliced
1 small leek, well washed and
trimmed

1 celery rib with leaves
1 small potato, peeled
Salt and freshly ground pepper
¼ teaspoon thyme
½ bay leaf
½ garlic clove
1 clove

1. Place all ingredients in a casserole with a cover.
2. Cover with water and bring to a boil.
3. Simmer 2 to 3 hours.
4. Serve the meat and vegetables separately. Use the liquid for soup or freeze it for another day.

COOKED BEEF SAUTE WITH ONIONS AND POTATOES

1 medium potato, peeled
Salt and freshly ground pepper
2 teaspoons of butter
2 onions, coarsely chopped

¼ pound cooked beef, thinly
sliced (use leftovers from roast
beef, boiled beef, soup)
½ garlic clove, minced
¼ teaspoon of wine vinegar
Minced parsley (optional)

1. Place the potato in cold water to cover. Salt and pepper and bring to a boil. Simmer 20 minutes, then drain.
2. Cut the potato in ¼-inch slices.
3. Melt the butter and add the potato slices and the onion. Cook 5 minutes.
4. Add the beef slices and cook another 10 minutes.
5. Sprinkle with garlic, vinegar, salt and pepper.
6. Serve hot with parsley garnish.

INDIVIDUAL MEAT LOAF—1

¼ pound ground round steak
1 egg
¼ teaspoon rosemary
  Salt and pepper
1 slice stale white bread, in
  crumbs

½ medium onion
½ red apple, 1 celery rib, or 1
  carrot
1 slice bacon

1. Break the meat into bits in a mixing bowl.
2. Add the egg, rosemary, salt, and pepper.
3. Add the bread crumbs to the seasoned meat. Put the onion and the apple, celery or carrot in a blender for one minute and add these to the meat.
4. Mix the ingredients well in the bowl and form into a ball.
5. Line a small skillet with aluminum foil and place loaf in the center; cover with bacon.
6. Bake for 45 minutes at 400 degrees.

INDIVIDUAL MEAT LOAF—2

¼ pound ground chuck or round
  steak (the size of a medium
  hamburger)
1 slice stale white bread, in
  crumbs
1 tablespoon green pepper,
  minced

2 tablespoons minced onion
1 egg
¼ teaspoon worcestershire sauce
1 teaspoon mustard
  Salt and pepper
1 tablespoon tomato paste
  (optional)

1. Place all ingredients in a bowl and mix well.
2. Form into a ball.
3. Line an ovenproof vessel with aluminum foil and place the meat loaf in the center.
4. Bake in a 350 degree oven for one hour. Let the loaf stand for 15 minutes before serving.

Note: Serve as is or with a sauce: tomato, mushroom, mustard, or use relish or ketchup.

INDIVIDUAL MEAT LOAF—3

¼ pound ground chuck steak
½ slice stale white bread, in crumbs
1 teaspoon peppercorns, crushed with a mortar and pestle

½ cup parsley, stems removed
1 egg yolk
Salt
2 tablespoons water

1. Preheat the oven to 350 degrees.
2. Use a blender to make bread crumbs; then use it to blend the parsley and water.
3. Mix all ingredients well in a bowl and form into a small loaf.
4. Place in an ovenproof pan lined with aluminum foil and bake 1 hour. Serve after letting the loaf stand ½ hour.

INDIVIDUAL MEAT LOAF WITH CARROTS

¼ pound ground round steak
2 tablespoons minced onion
1 egg
1 slice stale white bread, in crumbs

Pinch of thyme
Salt and pepper
3 carrots, sliced
1 cup beef broth

1. Mix all the ingredients except the carrots and broth, and mold into a small loaf.
2. Bake uncovered 1 hour in a 250 degree oven.
3. Boil carrots in the broth until tender.
4. Place loaf in the center of a warm plate; surround with the carrots.
5. Reduce broth by boiling to 2 tablespoons and pour over the meat.

GROUND BEEF AND MASHED POTATO LOAF

1 potato or enough to make 3 ounces of mashed potatoes
2 teaspoons butter
1 teaspoon cream
1 tablespoon chopped onion
¼ teaspoon minced garlic

3 ounces ground round steak
1 egg yolk
¼ teaspoon salt
¼ teaspoon black pepper
1 shake ground red pepper

1. Peel and slice the potato and boil in salted water until tender. Mash the cooked potato by passing it through a food mill or sieve. Then season with half the butter and the cream.
2. Sauté the onion and garlic in the remaining butter until the onion is translucent.
3. Crumble the ground round and add to the potatoes and then add the egg yolk, onion, garlic, salt, and black and red peppers and mix well.
4. Place in a well-buttered small casserole, or mold into a loaf, and bake in a 350-degree oven for 40 minutes.
5. Serve alone or with the following tomato sauce. Blend 1 teaspoon of flour into 1 teaspoon of butter. Add ¼ cup of milk over low heat, stirring with a wire whisk. When thickened, add 1 tablespoon of tomato paste and season to taste.

BEEF-HAM LOAF

¼ pound ground chuck steak
¼ cup ham, finely diced
1 slice stale bread
1 small onion, minced
3 tablespoons water

1 egg
¼ teaspoon rosemary
Salt and pepper
1 slice bacon

1. Break the meat into bits in a bowl and add the ham.

2. Crumble the bread into a blender and blend to fine crumbs. Mix into the meat.
3. Blend the onion and water in the blender and add to the meat with the egg, rosemary, salt and pepper. Mix well. Place in the freezer compartment of the refrigerator for 4 or 5 minutes. Remove and form into a small loaf with your hands.
4. Place the loaf in a small skillet or open pan which has been lined with aluminum foil. Cover the loaf with the strip of bacon, cut in half to make a better fit.
5. Bake for 45 minutes at 350 degrees and let stand ½ hour before serving.

FRUITY MEAT LOAF

4 tablespoons breadcrumbs	1 egg yolk
2 tablespoons chopped apple	2 tablespoons chopped onion
2 tablespoons chopped pear	¼ pound ground round steak
¼ teaspoon sage	Salt and pepper
⅛ teaspoon nutmeg	

1. Place the crumbs in a mixing bowl.
2. Put the apple and the pear in the blender with the sage and nutmeg. Blend to fine (about 3 seconds at high speed).
3. Add the egg yolk and blend 1 second longer.
4. Add the onion, meat, salt and pepper, and the fruit mixture to the mixing bowl. Knead and mix well by hand.
5. Place the mixture in an ovenproof pyrex muffin cup or other small vessel. Bake 1 hour and 15 minutes at 300 degrees.
6. Serve hot alone or with horseradish sauce or mustard.

HAMBURGER

¼ pound ground chuck or round	1 teaspoon parsley, chopped
Salt and freshly ground pepper	½ tablespoon butter
¼ teaspoon worcestershire sauce	¼ teaspoon lemon juice

1. Mold the ground beef into a patty, not too tightly compressed, in your hands.
2. Lightly salt the bottom of a skillet and heat it well.
3. Place the patty in the skillet, sear it on one side, and turn.
4. Reduce the heat and cook the patty to desired doneness. Three minutes on one side and about 2 minutes on the other will turn out a medium-rare hamburger if the fire is reduced to low. Pour the worcestershire sauce over it.
5. Remove the patty to a warm platter and garnish with parsley. Add the butter, pepper and lemon juice. Serve immediately.

FRENCHBURGER

1 teaspoon butter
¼ pound ground round steak

Salt and pepper
3 tablespoons red wine vinegar

1. Heat butter in a small frying pan.
2. Form meat into a patty, add salt and pepper, and brown well on both sides.
3. Remove meat to a small casserole, add wine vinegar, cover and cook over low heat 45 minutes.

HAMBURGER AU POIVRE

1 teaspoon oil
4 or 5 ounces ground chuck or round steak
Salt

1 teaspoon freshly ground pepper
1 tablespoon cognac

1. Oil a skillet and heat it well.
2. Mold the ground meat into a patty using your hands. On a sheet of wax paper, mix the salt and pepper and press the patty into

the mixture, first one side and then the other. Sear both sides of the meat in the hot oil.

3. Cook the hamburger to desired doneness; 3 minutes on each side for rare.
4. Pour off the excess grease from the cooking pan and add the cognac. Stir well and pour over the patty. Serve hot.

GROUND MEAT PATTY WITH CREAM SAUCE

¼ pound ground chuck steak	1 teaspoon butter
1 slice bacon, diced	3 tablespoons light cream
Salt and freshly ground pepper	1 teaspoon brandy
⅛ teaspoon nutmeg	1 teaspoon lemon juice
1 teaspoon flour	

1. Place the beef in a bowl and separate loosely; add the diced bacon and mix well.
2. Season with salt, pepper, and nutmeg. Blend together well and shape into a patty.
3. Dust the patty with flour and prepare the skillet by melting the butter. Over medium heat, brown each side of the patty. Reduce the heat and simmer to desired doneness.
4. Remove the patty from the skillet and pour off most of the fat.
5. Add the cream and cook to reduce to half the quantity. Add the lemon juice and brandy. Mix well. Pour the sauce over the patty and serve immediately.

MEATBALLS—1

¼ pound ground chuck or round steak	¼ teaspoon grated lemon rind
1 egg yolk	⅛ teaspoon grated nutmeg
¼ teaspoon parsley, chopped	Salt and pepper
¼ slice stale white bread, in crumbs	Flour
	1 tablespoon oil

1. In a small bowl mix all ingredients except the oil and flour. Blend well with a fork and the fingers. Form into 4 balls.
2. Sprinkle flour on a sheet of wax paper and roll the balls until they are well coated with flour.
3. Pour the oil into a small skillet and brown the meatballs on all sides over a moderate flame.
4. Continue cooking until done (about 15 minutes, adding butter if required to prevent sticking).

Note: The meatballs may also be added to tomato sauce after Step 3. In that case, simmer for ½ hour in sauce before serving.

MEATBALLS—2

¼ pound lean ground beef	2 dashes worcestershire sauce
½ teaspoon salt	2 tablespoons finely chopped
½ garlic clove, grated	parsley
2 tablespoons finely grated onion	1 tablespoon vegetable oil

1. Mix all ingredients except the oil in a bowl and form into balls the size of a walnut, about 6 balls.
2. Melt the oil in a frying pan and cook the balls quickly to a golden brown on the exterior. Do not overcook. Rare is recommended, but the meatballs may be cooked to your choice of doneness (about 5 minutes for medium).
3. Serve the balls warm. They are good alone or with your favorite sauce: tomato, lemon juice, etc.

SPANISH MEATBALLS

¼ pound ground round steak
2 small onions, chopped (about 4 tablespoons)
1 tablespoon tomato paste
  Salt
⅛ teaspoon ground red pepper
2 teaspoons vegetable oil

1 garlic clove, minced
2 tablespoons raw rice
1 tomato, peeled, cored, and diced
½ cup chicken broth
½ teaspoon saffron

1. Mix well the ground meat, one of the chopped onions, tomato paste, salt, and pepper and form into four small balls.
2. In 1 teaspoon of the oil, brown the balls and let cook 5 minutes. Set aside.
3. In the remaining teaspoon of oil sauté the other onion and the garlic until wilted.
4. Add the rice and cook, stirring, for a minute or so.
5. Now add the chopped tomato, salt, chicken broth, and saffron. Bring to a boil and simmer 20 minutes or until the rice is done.
6. Add the meatballs, cover and cook another minute or so. Serve hot.

MEATBALLS STROGANOFF

¼ pound ground chuck steak
1 egg yolk
1 tablespoon breadcrumbs
1 tablespoon milk
  Salt and freshly ground pepper
  Pinch ground nutmeg
½ tablespoon paprika
½ tablespoon butter

1 ounce (about 4 medium-sized) mushrooms, thinly sliced
1 tablespoon chopped onion
1 tablespoon dry sherry
1 tablespoon light cream
¼ cup sour cream

1. Place the ground meat in a bowl and add the egg yolk.

2. Soak the breadcrumbs in milk and add to the meat. Add the salt, pepper, and nutmeg. Mix well and form into about five balls, 1½ inches in diameter.
3. Sprinkle the paprika on a sheet of wax paper and roll the balls in the seasoning to coat on all sides.
4. In a small skillet, melt the butter and brown the balls on all sides for about 5 minutes over medium heat. Add the mushrooms and onion and cook a minute or so, partially covered.
5. Add the sherry and cream. Cook about ten minutes, partially covered.
6. Stir in the sour cream. Bring just to a boil and serve.

BEEF CURRY

¼ pound ground chuck	½ bay leaf
¼ teaspoon salt	¼ teaspoon crushed red pepper
¼ teaspoon freshly ground black pepper	2 teaspoons butter
	⅓ cup chopped onion
1 teaspoon vinegar	¼ cup chopped green pepper
1 tablespoon curry powder	¼ cup milk
½ garlic clove, crushed	¼ teaspoon lemon juice

1. Mix together the meat, salt, pepper, vinegar, curry powder, garlic, bay leaf, and red pepper. Let stand 2 hours or more.
2. Melt the butter and sauté the onion and green pepper for several minutes, stirring occasionally.
3. Stir in the meat mixture, cover, and cook slowly for 45 minutes, either in the oven or on top of the stove over a flame tamer.
4. Add the milk and continue cooking for 10 to 15 minutes.
5. Sprinkle with lemon juice just before serving.

CURRIED BEEF WITH PEAS

1 teaspoon butter	¼ teaspoon coriander
2 tablespoons chopped onion	4 shakes crushed red pepper
¼ pound ground chuck	⅓ cup canned tomatoes
Salt and pepper	⅓ cup fresh or frozen peas
¼ teaspoon curry powder	

1. Melt the butter and cook the onions for 2 minutes or until they wilt.
2. Add the ground meat, salt, pepper, curry powder, coriander, and red pepper. Cook about 5 minutes, stirring and breaking up the meat with a wooden spoon.
3. Add the tomatoes and simmer 20 minutes.
4. Add the peas and cook until they are tender. If you use frozen peas, this will not take long.

Note: This dish may be prepared ahead of time and reheated just before serving. Add the peas at the last.

STIR-FRIED GROUND BEEF AND VEGETABLES

1 teaspoon oil	¼ teaspoon cornstarch
1 onion, chopped (half a cup)	1 tablespoon water
¼ cup chopped green pepper	2 tablespoons sherry
3 ounces ground chuck	1 tablespoon soy sauce
4 cherry tomatoes, quartered, or ½ cup diced tomatoes	Salt and pepper

1. Heat the oil over medium heat in a skillet and add the onion and green pepper. Sauté until the onion becomes translucent, stirring constantly.
2. Stir in the ground beef, breaking it up into bits in the process.

Continue the constant stirring until the meat loses its reddish color.

3. Add the tomatoes and continue the agitated cooking for several minutes until the tomatoes appear soft.

4. Mix together the cornstarch and water and stir into the meat and vegetable mixture.

5. Stir in the sherry, soy sauce, salt, and pepper and serve hot.

Note: This dish is inspired by the Chinese cooking method of "stir frying" in which a wok and special spatula are employed. For this limited quantity, a skillet and spoon will suffice. Just remember to stir constantly over medium heat.

GROUND BEEF, CELERY, AND TOMATOES

1 tablespoon of oil	1 cup chopped celery
1 onion, chopped	½ cup tomatoes, chopped, peeled,
Salt and pepper	and cored, or the same quantity
¼ pound ground chuck steak	of canned tomatoes

1. Heat the oil in a small casserole or covered sauce pan and sauté the chopped onion until it wilts, stirring to prevent burning.

2. Stir in the salt, pepper, and ground meat in bits and continue stirring to reduce the size of the bits further.

3. When the meat changes its red color to gray, add the celery and tomatoes and mix well.

4. Cover the casserole and simmer ½ hour or until the celery is done to your taste.

GROUND BEEF AND PEPPERS

1   teaspoon cooking oil
½   cup chopped green pepper
½   cup chopped onion

¼   pound ground chuck or round
     steak
     Salt and pepper

1. Pour the oil into a small casserole and over a medium flame sauté the green pepper and onion, stirring to prevent browning. Continue cooking until the onion becomes translucent, about 4 minutes.
2. Add the chopped meat in bits and cook, stirring to break up the meat into smaller pieces. Continue cooking several minutes until the meat changes color and is mixed well with the onion and green pepper.
3. Add salt and pepper, stir again, cover and simmer ½ hour using a flame tamer or very low heat. Serve warm or let stand until you are ready to eat and reheat.

GROUND BEEF AND STEWED TOMATOES

1   teaspoon vegetable oil
1   small onion, minced
1   garlic clove, finely chopped

¼   pound ground round steak
     Salt and pepper
1   8½-ounce can stewed tomatoes

1. Heat oil in a small skillet and sauté onion and garlic over low heat for 10 minutes.
2. Add ground beef, salt, and pepper; separate beef with a spoon and cook about 10 minutes or until the meat loses its red color.
3. Add tomatoes to the beef; mix well, chopping the tomatoes with your spoon until fine.
4. Simmer uncovered about 1 hour or until the liquid has evaporated. Serve with rice or boiled potatoes.

BEEF PICADILLO

2 tablespoons raisins
2 tablespoons sherry wine
1 teaspoon olive oil
½ garlic clove, minced
2 tablespoons chopped onion
¼ pound ground chuck
Salt and freshly ground pepper

⅓ cup canned tomatoes, passed through a sieve to remove the seeds
1 teaspoon vinegar
⅛ teaspoon cumin
1 clove

1. Soak the raisins in the sherry for ½ hour or more.
2. Heat the oil and add the garlic, onion, and beef. Stir constantly and cook for 4 minutes.
3. Add the salt and pepper, tomatoes, vinegar, cumin, clove, and raisins and bring to a boil. Simmer 30 minutes and serve hot with rice.

PICADILLO

1 teaspoon vegetable oil
½ garlic clove, minced
1 tablespoon chopped onion
5 ounces ground chuck
Salt and freshly ground pepper

½ cup canned tomatoes
1 tablespoon vinegar
1 tablespoon pickled chilies (jalapeños), minced
Pinch ground cumin

1. Heat the oil and sauté the garlic and onion for 1 minute.
2. Add the beef and stir well. Cook for 5 minutes, stirring frequently.
3. Add the remaining ingredients and bring to a boil; lower heat and simmer 30 minutes.

Note: The above quantity of chilies is moderately hot to my taste. Adjust to your own tolerance.

GROUND BEEF WITH DILL

¼ pound ground chuck, round, or other cut of beef
1 teaspoon ground dill weed
Salt and pepper

1 teaspoon butter
2 drops worcestershire sauce
6 drops lemon juice

1. Mix well ground beef, dill, salt and pepper and mold into a patty. Don't use much salt here, since the patty is cooked on a light bed of salt.
2. Salt and heat a small skillet and cook the patty three minutes on each side, pressing down with a spatula from time to time and moving the patty to keep it from sticking.
3. Remove the meat to a warm plate and serve hot with the butter, worcestershire sauce, and lemon juice on top.

CHILI

½ cup chopped onion
1 garlic clove, minced
1 teaspoon vegetable oil
¼ pound ground chuck or round steak
¼ teaspoon salt
2 teaspoons chili powder
¼ teaspoon crushed red pepper (this is hot; use to your taste)

½ teaspoon ground cumin
1 teaspoon oregano
½ cup tomato puree or canned tomatoes passed through a sieve to remove the seeds
2 tablespoons tomato paste
½ cup canned kidney beans

1. Wilt the onion and garlic in the oil. Stir and cook a minute or so without burning.
2. Add the meat, stirring to separate, and mix it well with the vegetables.
3. Now add the salt, chili powder, red pepper, ground cumin, and oregano and stir again.

4. Add the tomatoes and tomato paste and simmer 1 hour or longer.
5. Simmer the beans in their juice for several minutes and add to the chili.
6. Serve hot with a topping of shredded lettuce, chopped stuffed olives, and chopped onion or your favorite relish (optional).

Note: This dish can be prepared the day before and reheated at serving time.

CHILI WITH TOMATO PASTE

1   teaspoon vegetable oil
½   cup chopped onion
1   garlic clove, minced
3½ ounces ground chuck steak
2   tablespoons tomato paste

¼   teaspoon crushed red pepper
1   teaspoon chili powder
¼   teaspoon salt
½   cup kidney beans with 2 teaspoons liquid from the can

1. In the oil, sauté the onions and garlic for 3 minutes, stirring.
2. Add the chuck and stir to break up the pieces. Continue cooking until the meat changes color, about 2 minutes.
3. Now add the tomato paste and seasonings and stir to blend.
4. Add the beans and liquid, stir again, and simmer at least 1 hour. Serve hot.

POTATO AND CHILI CASSEROLE

½   garlic clove, minced
2   tablespoons chopped onion
1¼ teaspoons vegetable oil
¼   pound ground chuck steak
½   cup canned tomatoes, sieved to remove seeds

½   teaspoon chili powder
    Salt and pepper (preferably hot pepper)
2   small potatoes (4 ounces), in ¼-inch slices

1. Cook the garlic and onion in one teaspoon of the oil for 3 minutes, stirring constantly.
2. Add the meat and continue cooking and stirring until the meat changes color.
3. Add the tomatoes, chili powder, salt and pepper and mix well.
4. Cook over low heat for 1 hour.
5. Oil a small baking dish and put in potatoes.
6. Pour the chili over the potatoes and cover.
7. Simmer over a flame tamer until the potatoes are tender to the touch of a fork.

CHILI MAC

1 teaspoon oil	1 teaspoon tomato paste
¼ cup chopped onion	Salt and pepper
¼ teaspoon minced garlic	1 shake crushed red pepper
3 ounces ground round steak	1 teaspoon chili powder
1 8-ounce can of Italian plum tomatoes	2 cups water
	¼ cup macaroni

1. Oil a small skillet and sauté the onion and garlic until the onion is translucent.
2. Add the ground round and cook, stirring, over medium heat until the meat loses its red color.
3. Pass the tomatoes through a sieve to remove the seeds, and add to the cooking meat.
4. Season with tomato paste, salt, peppers, and chili powder. Place on a flame tamer over low heat.
5. Cook the macaroni for 7 minutes in vigorously boiling water with a little salt added. Drain in a colander.
6. Add the drained macaroni to the meat sauce and continue simmering until serving time, at least 15 minutes.

Note: Do not let the chili become too dry. Add water as necessary to keep a nice consistency.

CHILI, TEX-MEX VARIETY

1 teaspoon vegetable oil
¼ pound beef chuck, cubed
1 tablespoon chili powder
1 teaspoon flour
1 teaspoon garlic, crushed or finely chopped

½ teaspoon ground cumin
1 teaspoon oregano
  Salt and pepper
  Crushed red pepper (optional)
¼ cup beef broth

1. Heat the oil and brown the beef lightly in a casserole with cover.
2. Add the chili powder, flour, garlic, cumin, oregano, salt and pepper and stir well to coat the meat.
3. Pour in the broth and mix well. Bring to a boil and cover. Cook over low heat, using a flame tamer, for 2 or 3 hours. Stir occasionally.

Note: Serve in a ring of grits or rice when very hot. (The chili can be saved in the refrigerator several days and reheated before serving.)

HOT TAMALE PIE

1 teaspoon vegetable oil
1 small onion, chopped
1 garlic clove, minced
3 ounces ground chuck steak
1 tablespoon tomato paste
¼ teaspoon crushed red pepper
1 teaspoon chili powder
½ teaspoon salt

½ cup kidney beans
¼ cup cornmeal
1 teaspoon flour
1 teaspoon sugar
½ teaspoon baking powder
1 egg yolk
2 tablespoons milk

1. Sauté the onion and garlic in the oil for a minute or so and add the ground meat. Stir and cook until the red is gone from the meat.
2. Add the tomato paste, red pepper, chili powder, half the salt,

and beans, with about 2 tablespoons of the liquid from the can.
3. Simmer 1 hour, covered.
4. Sift together the cornmeal, flour, sugar, remaining salt, and baking powder, and add the egg yolk and milk. Mix well and pour over the chili mixture. Smooth it over the chili and place in a 425 degree oven for 20 minutes.
5. Let cool 5 minutes and serve.

SCALLOPED POTATOES AND HAMBURGER

¼	pound ground round steak	1	tablespoon minced onion
1	teaspoon oil	¼	cup milk
2	small potatoes, sliced		Salt and pepper
1	tablespoon flour		

1. Mold ground meat into 4 small patties and brown in oil.
2. Place patties in a small casserole and cover with sliced potatoes. Dust potatoes with the flour; add onion and milk, salt and pepper.
3. Cook covered in a 300 degree oven for 30 minutes, uncover and continue cooking until potatoes are well browned.

MACARONI-BEEF MEDLEY

½	cup macaroni	¼	teaspoon oregano
1	tablespoon oil	4	ounces ground chuck steak
1	garlic clove, minced	⅓	cup tomato sauce
⅓	cup chopped onion		Grated Parmesan cheese
	Salt and freshly ground pepper		(about 2 tablespoons)

1. Bring a quart of water to a boil with 1 teaspoon salt.
2. Add the macaroni and boil 6 minutes. Drain and flush with cold water in a colander.
3. Heat the oil in a small casserole and sauté the garlic and onion until the onion becomes translucent.
4. Add the salt, pepper, and oregano. Stir.
5. Break the ground steak into small pieces and add. Stir and continue breaking into smaller pieces, cooking until the meat changes color.
6. Add the tomato sauce and mix well.
7. Stir in the cooked macaroni, top with cheese, and bake at 350 degrees for 20 minutes. Serve hot with more cheese if desired.

EGGPLANT AND BEEF CASSEROLE

1 cup peeled and diced eggplant	1 cup canned tomatoes
1 tablespoon vegetable oil	Salt and pepper
¼ cup minced onion	1 teaspoon sugar
¼ cup chopped green pepper	½ cup breadcrumbs
3½ ounces chopped chuck or ground round	½ cup grated sharp cheese

1. Sauté eggplant in oil with the onion, green pepper, and ground beef for 10 minutes, stirring.
2. Add the tomatoes, salt, pepper, and sugar. Mix well and continue cooking another 10 minutes.
3. Pour into a greased casserole and cover with the breadcrumbs and cheese. Bake at 400 degrees for 20 minutes.

GROUND MEAT CASSEROLE

1 teaspoon vegetable oil
3 ounces ground chuck or round
  steak
1 small onion, chopped
½ cup chopped green pepper
3 stuffed olives
4 ounces canned tomatoes

1 tablespoon worcestershire
  sauce
¼ teaspoon crushed red pepper
  Salt
½ cup cooked pasta (spaghetti
  or macaroni)
½ cup grated cheese
½ cup breadcrumbs

1. Cook all ingredients except the cheese and breadcrumbs in the oil, stirring constantly.
2. Place in a small casserole, top with cheese and crumbs and bake 25 minutes at 350 degrees.

ZUCCHINI-BEEF CASSEROLE

1 medium zucchini, in ½-inch
  slices
2 tablespoons flour
1 tablespoon olive oil
1 tablespoon butter
¼ cup chopped onion
1 garlic clove, minced
3 ounces ground chuck steak
  Salt and freshly ground pepper
⅓ cup tomato sauce

1 bay leaf
1 pinch oregano
¼ cup red wine
1 pinch parsley
2 tablespoons chopped
  mushrooms
  Bechamel sauce (see
  instructions below)
3 tablespoons grated Parmesan
  cheese

1. Let the zucchini stand in cold salted water for 10 minutes. Drain, rinse, and dry.
2. Dredge the zucchini in the flour, brown in hot oil, and drain.
3. Heat half the butter and cook the onion and garlic to a golden brown. Add the meat, stir, and cook about 10 minutes. Add the salt, pepper, tomato sauce, bay leaf, oregano, wine, and parsley. Stir and cook until most of the liquid has evaporated.

4. Sauté the mushrooms in the remaining butter until golden and add.
5. Butter a small casserole and place half the zucchini in the bottom; top with the meat mixture and the other half of the zucchini. Cover with the Bechamel sauce and top with cheese. Bake 30 minutes at 400 degrees or until golden.
6. Remove from the oven and let stand ½ hour before serving.

Bechamel Sauce

Melt 1 tablespoon of butter and blend in 1 tablespoon of flour; add ⅔ cup of milk and ¼ cup of cream all at once and stir with a wire whisk to mix well. Cook 5 minutes and cool a little. To 1 egg yolk add a little of the blended flour and butter and mix well; pour the egg mix into the remaining sauce and stir well; simmer and set aside.

STUFFED ZUCCHINI

1 medium zucchini	1 cracker, in crumbs
1 teaspoon butter	1½ tablespoons grated Parmesan
¼ cup chopped onion	cheese
1 garlic clove, minced	1 tablespoon heavy cream
3½ ounces ground round steak	1 shake crushed red pepper
¼ teaspoon rosemary	1 ounce vermouth or dry white
Salt and pepper	wine
1 tablespoon tomato paste	

1. Cut off ends of the zucchini, slice in half, and scoop out the flesh with a melon ball cutter or small spoon in order to make shells. Retain the flesh.
2. Melt the butter in a small frying pan and add the zucchini flesh, onion, and garlic. Stir and cook until the onion is translucent, about 2 minutes.

3. Add the ground round and stir and cook until the meat loses its red color.
4. Stir in the rosemary, salt, pepper, and tomato paste. Keep stirring and add the cracker crumbs, Parmesan cheese, cream, and red pepper.
5. Stuff the zucchini shells with the seasoned mixture. Place them in a suitable small baking dish or small frying pan, add the vermouth, and bake uncovered at 350 degrees for 40 minutes or until the zucchini shells are tender to the touch of a fork.

GROUND BEEF STEW WITHOUT WATER

¼ teaspoon vegetable oil
1 garlic clove, pressed or finely chopped
¼ pound ground chuck steak
  Salt and pepper
1 or 2 small white onions, peeled
1 tablespoon dry split peas or lentils or barley (optional)

2 medium carrots, sliced
1 very small potato, peeled and halved
¼ teaspoon ground thyme
2 small tomatoes, cored and halved

1. Put the oil in a small casserole with cover and heat over low heat. Stir in the garlic and slowly add the ground chuck. Cook until the meat has lost its reddish color.
2. Salt and pepper the casserole, and add the dry peas or lentils at this point. Continue cooking and stirring.
3. Add the onion, carrots, potato, and thyme. Cover the other ingredients with the halved tomatoes, cut side down. Add a little salt and cover tightly.
4. Let the casserole steam and cook on top of the stove over a very low flame until the carrots are tender, 1 to 2 hours. When tender turn off the heat. Warm up at serving time.

GROUND BEEF STEW

1 teaspoon vegetable oil	½ stalk celery, sliced
1 small onion, diced	1 small potato, peeled and diced
1 garlic clove, minced	1 tablespoon tomato paste
¼ pound ground chuck	Salt and pepper
2 small carrots, sliced	½ cup water

1. Heat the oil in a small casserole and add the garlic and onion. Cook over low heat for 2 minutes.
2. Break the meat into small pieces, add, and stir until the meat has lost its red color.
3. Add the carrots, celery, potato, tomato paste, salt, pepper, and water.
4. Bring to a boil, turn down heat, then cover and simmer 1 hour or until the carrots and potatoes are tender. Serve in a soup bowl or with rice.

Veal

Blanquette of Veal • Veal and Vegetables
Veal with Dill and Celery • Veal in White Wine
Veal with Shallots and Wine • Veal and Bacon Rolls
Veal Birds • Veal Chop Creole
Scallopini of Veal • Veal Sauté in Tomato Sauce
Veal Marsala

Veal came to my attention when, as a child, I heard my aunt, who had just returned from a social gathering, criticize the chicken salad, saying: "I think the salad contained some veal." In those days that meant that the cook had extended the chicken with a cheaper portion of veal. Imagine that, with the price of veal as high as it is today! Prices have changed so radically, now one could well extend the veal with chicken and help the budget.

The possibility of substituting veal for chicken is a real one because veal and the white meat of chicken have a delicate, bland flavor that lends itself happily to seasonings and sauces; however, there is character in each meat and neither need be disguised.

At times it is difficult to find the best veal in local markets, but one doesn't have to go to Rome either. The search for tender fresh veal is worth the try. I do just this frequently and I recommend a few of my favorite recipes in these pages.

BLANQUETTE OF VEAL

½ pound veal, in 1-inch cubes
   Salt and pepper
1 bay leaf
¼ teaspoon parsley flakes

1 onion, peeled and stuck with
   two cloves
2 carrots, quartered
1 tablespoon butter
1 tablespoon flour

1. Place the meat in a deep saucepan and cover with water. Cook about 6 minutes, skimming off the foam.
2. Add the salt, pepper, bay leaf, parsley, onion, and carrots. Cover and cook 1½ hours or until the meat is tender.
3. Remove meat and vegetables to a warm bowl.
4. Strain the liquid and reduce by boiling until about ½ cup remains.
5. Blend the flour and butter and add a little at a time to the liquid until desired thickness is obtained. Pour this sauce over the meat and vegetables. Serve hot.

Note: Serve with rice.

VEAL AND VEGETABLES

½ pound veal neck or breast
   meat, in ¼-inch cubes
½ onion, chopped
½ green pepper, chopped
1 carrot, sliced

¼ teaspoon sugar
1 tablespon butter
1 tablespoon flour
   Salt and pepper

1. Place all ingredients except the flour and butter in a saucepan, add water to cover, and simmer 1 hour or until the meat is tender.
2. Melt the butter in a small pyrex bowl and stir in the flour.
3. Add the butter-flour mixture to the stew a little at a time, stirring with a wire whisk until the desired consistency is reached.
4. Serve hot with rice.

VEAL WITH DILL AND CELERY

1 tablespoon butter	1 tablespoon flour
½ pound veal, in ½-inch cubes	¼ teaspoon sugar
Salt and pepper	½ cup chicken broth
½ garlic clove, minced	½ cup diced celery
2 tablespoons minced onion	¼ cup heavy cream
1 teaspoon dried dill weed or 1 tablespoon chopped fresh dill	

1. Melt the butter in a small casserole and add veal, salt, pepper, garlic, onion, and dill and cook stirring for 4 minutes. Do not brown.
2. Sprinkle the veal with flour and sugar and add half the broth. Stir, cover, and simmer 1 hour.
3. Cook the celery until tender in the remaining chicken broth and add to the casserole.
4. Add the cream and bring to a boil, stirring to mix well. Serve immediately.

Note: Other vegetables may be substituted for celery. Try carrots, leeks, or peas.

VEAL IN WHITE WINE

2 tablespoons vegetable oil	2 tablespoons onion or shallots, finely chopped
½ pound veal, in ½-inch cubes (a small cutlet or stew veal will do; freeze any extra veal)	⅛ cup white wine
Salt and pepper	¼ cup chicken broth
1 tablespoon butter	3 tablespoons heavy cream
	¼ teaspoon minced parsley

1. Heat the oil in a skillet to hot; sprinkle the veal cubes with salt and pepper and add to the skillet.

2. Stir the veal in the hot oil to prevent browning and cook for 2 minutes.
3. Remove the veal to a warm dish and wipe out the skillet.
4. Add the butter to the clean skillet and put in the onion or shallots. Stir; do not brown. After a minute or so add the wine and let the liquid evaporate almost completely before adding the chicken broth. Continue cooking and stirring until the liquid is reduced to about 1 tablespoon.
5. Drain any liquid accumulated from the meat into the skillet and cook another minute or so. Add the cream and stir; follow with the meat and bring to a boil. Serve hot with chopped parsley.

VEAL WITH SHALLOTS AND WINE

1 tablespoon butter	2 tablespoons chopped shallots
¼ pound veal, thinly sliced (scallopini)	¼ cup white wine
	Salt and pepper

1. Melt the butter in a small skillet and sauté the veal for about 5 minutes.
2. Remove the veal and keep warm. Add the chopped shallots to the skillet and cook until wilted over low heat.
3. Pour the wine into skillet and boil, scraping the bottom and sides of the skillet to dissolve any clinging particles. Add salt and pepper to taste. Reduce to a rather thick sauce and spoon over the veal or return the veal to the pan for a few seconds to warm it up before serving.

VEAL AND BACON ROLLS

¼ pound veal, thinly sliced and cut into bacon-width strips

4 slices bacon (one slice for each veal strip)

1 tablespoon chopped shallots

¼ cup white wine

1. Place each veal strip on 1 slice of bacon and roll into a ball. Secure the roll with a toothpick.
2. Over low heat sauté the bacon rolls about 5 minutes on each side. Move the rolls occasionally to prevent sticking. Remove the rolls and keep warm.
3. Pour out most of the grease in the pan, leaving a small amount to sauté the shallots.
4. When the shallots are tender, after about 2 minutes, add the wine and boil to reduce the sauce by half.
5. Return the rolls to the sauce, heat well, and serve.

VEAL BIRDS

(If you have ever cooked quail with bacon, and made a gravy, this dish will remind you of it.)

½ pound veal, about ½-inch thick

3 strips bacon

¼ teaspoon oil

Salt and pepper

1 teaspoon flour

¼ cup cream

1. Trim the veal of any excess fat and cut it into 3 equal pieces as round as possible.
2. Wrap the bacon slices around the veal pieces and secure the bacon in place with toothpicks.
3. Oil the bottom of a casserole and brown the veal and bacon on both sides.

4. Cover the casserole and cook on top of the stove over low heat or in the oven at 300 degrees for 45 minutes or until the veal is tender to a fork. Salt and pepper to taste.
5. Remove the veal and bacon from the casserole and drain all but 1 tablespoon of the fat from the casserole. Stir in the flour and pour in the cream. Continue stirring until the sauce is smooth and beginning to thicken. Return the "birds" to the casserole and cover. Keep warm and serve hot by turning up the fire just before the final moment.

VEAL CHOP CREOLE

5 ounces veal	$\frac{1}{8}$ teaspoon minced garlic
Salt and pepper	$\frac{1}{2}$ cup canned tomatoes, cut into
$\frac{1}{3}$ cup chopped onion	small pieces
$\frac{1}{8}$ cup chopped green pepper	$\frac{1}{4}$ teaspoon thyme
$\frac{1}{4}$ cup chopped celery	$\frac{1}{4}$ teaspoon minced parsley

1. Salt and pepper the meat and place in a small casserole with cover.
2. Mix the other ingredients and add.
3. Cover and bake in 300-degree oven for 1 hour.
4. Uncover and continue baking for 20 minutes longer.
5. Serve with the sauce which is ample but good.

SCALLOPINI OF VEAL

4	to 5 ounces of veal leg, thinly sliced	½	garlic clove, minced
1	tablespoon flour	1	tablespoon chopped onion
	Salt and pepper	¼	teaspoon rosemary
1	tablespoon butter	¼	teaspoon minced parsley
1	teaspoon olive oil	¼	cup marsala wine
		¼	cup diced tomatoes

1. Cut the veal in serving pieces, about 4, and place between 2 layers of wax paper. Pound veal very thin with a mallet or the bottom of a skillet.
2. Dredge the veal in a mixture of flour, salt, and pepper.
3. Heat the butter and oil in a skillet and brown the veal on both sides. Remove to a warm casserole or covered skillet and keep warm.
4. Add the garlic to the skillet where the veal was cooked, then add the onion, rosemary, and parsley. Stir and cook a minute or so.
5. Add the wine and tomatoes and stir well. Add the veal and cover. Cook to tender, about 5 minutes. Serve veal with the sauce on top.

VEAL SAUTE IN TOMATO SAUCE

	Salt and pepper	1	teaspoon flour
1	veal chop or about 3 or 4 ounces of veal trimmed of fat and bone, in cubes	1	tablespoon white wine or vermouth
½	teaspoon vegetable oil	1	tablespoon tomato paste
¼	cup chopped onion	2	tablespoons chicken broth
¼	garlic clove, minced	¼	teaspoon rosemary, finely chopped
	A pinch of saffron		

1. Preheat the oven to 375 degrees.
2. Salt and pepper the veal and brown in the oil on all sides.
3. Add the onion, garlic, and saffron and cook another minute or so.
4. Stir in the flour and mix well.
5. Now add the wine, tomato paste, and broth. Stir well.
6. Stir in the chopped rosemary, cover and bake 40 minutes.

VEAL MARSALA

1 thin scallop veal, about ¼-inch thick and ¼ pound in weight or two smaller pieces weighing the same

1 teaspoon butter
Salt and pepper
2 tablespoons marsala wine

1. Place the veal between 2 layers of wax paper and pound with a mallet or heavy skillet until very thin.
2. Melt the butter in a skillet and cook the veal 3 minutes on each side over medium heat.
3. Salt and pepper the veal and pour the marsala over it. Stir well, turn, and remove the veal to a warm plate.
4. Agitate the liquid remaining in the skillet to absorb the particles that have formed during cooking and pour the sauce over the veal. Serve immediately.

Lamb

Braised Roast Lamb • Braised Lamb with Eggplant
Lamb Steak with Tarragon Cream Gravy
Pan-Broiled Lamb Chop with Fresh Tomatoes
Curried Lamb Shank with Lentils • Lamb Curry
Lamb Stew • Lamb and Rice Stew • Dilled Lamb Stew
Lamb Stew French-Style • Hotpot
Lamb and Eggplant Casserole • Curried Lamb with Lentils

Whenever the menu says "roast leg of lamb, minted peach," as it does frequently on Saturday in a local restaurant, I am reminded of Aunt Sally's traditional Easter dinner of roast leg of lamb, mint sauce, cooked in the fireless cooker while we were at church. It was worth waiting for, worth even waiting another year.

I have prepared roast leg of lamb many times in my kitchen. It is good with just salt, pepper, and garlic and the minimum cooking time. However I have always had more pleasure in making something more complicated with the willing meat of the lamb. I mean lamb in casseroles and stews. I have found these dishes come out with more goodness than the component parts indicated in advance. This mystery and surprise factor never ceases to interest me.

BRAISED ROAST LAMB

4 ounces lean lamb, in ½-inch cubes
1 tablespoon vegetable oil or butter
1 tablespoon chopped onion
1 carrot, chopped
1 small garlic clove, sliced
½ bay leaf
  Salt and pepper
½ cup beef broth
1 tablespoon chili sauce
1 tablespoon chopped parsley

1. Sear the lamb in the oil in a small casserole and remove to a warm platter.
2. Add to the casserole the onion, carrot, and garlic. Cook a few minutes.
3. Return the meat to the casserole. Add the remaining ingredients. Simmer 2 hours.
4. Remove the meat and vegetables from the casserole and reduce the sauce to about ¼ cup. If desired, thicken with 1 teaspoon of flour shaken together with 1 teaspoon of water in a glass jar.

BRAISED LAMB WITH EGGPLANT

½ garlic clove, minced
1 tablespoon vegetable oil
10 ounces boned lamb
  Salt and freshly ground pepper
½ cup cherry tomatoes, diced, or canned Italian plum tomatoes, diced
½ bay leaf
⅛ teaspoon thyme
⅓ cup chopped scallions or small white onions
½ teaspoon lemon juice
1 cup diced eggplant
1 tablespoon butter, melted
1 teaspoon chopped parsley

1. Sauté the garlic in oil for a minute or so. Sprinkle the meat with salt and pepper and brown on both sides in the oil with the garlic.
2. Add the tomatoes, bay leaf, thyme, and onion. Pour the lemon juice over, cover and cook over moderate heat for ½ hour.

3. Arrange the eggplant on top of the stew, pour over the butter, add salt, pepper, and parsley and cover. Continue cooking until the meat and eggplant are tender (about 20 minutes).
4. Serve the meat and vegetables over rice and reduce the liquid to a small amount by boiling rapidly for a few minutes.

LAMB STEAK WITH TARRAGON CREAM GRAVY

10 ounces lamb, sliced from the leg
Salt and pepper
1 teaspoon dried tarragon
1 medium onion

½ garlic clove
1 teaspoon flour
3 tablespoons boiling water
1 tablespoon heavy cream

1. Preheat the oven to 450 degrees.
2. Place the lamb slice in a shallow roasting vessel, sprinkle with salt, pepper and tarragon. Cut the onion in quarters and place in the pan. Slice the garlic and rub the meat with the cut pieces. Discard the garlic.
3. Roast the meat for 10 minutes, then reduce the heat to 350 degrees. Cook another 20 minutes. Remove the lamb and let it stand while preparing the gravy.
4. Pour off any excess fat from the roasting pan and add the flour. Stir and mix well. Add the water and blend well, dissolving the brown particles on the bottom of the pan. Add more water if the gravy is too thick.
5. Stir in the cream and serve over the lamb after testing for seasoning. You may want to add more salt.

PAN-BROILED LAMB CHOP WITH FRESH TOMATOES

Salt and pepper
1 teaspoon vegetable oil
1 lamb chop

½ cup fresh tomatoes, peeled, seeded, and finely chopped

1. Heat the oil to hot in a heavy skillet.
2. Salt and pepper the chop and cook it 5 minutes on each side until brown over medium heat.
3. Reduce the heat and continue cooking another minute or so on each side.
4. Remove the chop from the skillet and keep it warm. Pour off all the grease in the skillet and add the tomatoes. Stir and cook about 2 minutes and serve over the chop on a warm plate. Add more salt and pepper if desired.

CURRIED LAMB SHANK WITH LENTILS

1 small lamb shank or ½ pound leg of lamb meat, in cubes	¼ teaspoon turmeric
1 teaspoon vegetable oil	1 teaspoon poppy seeds
1 garlic clove, minced	Salt and pepper
1 small onion, minced	½ cup water
¼ teaspoon curry powder	4 tablespoons lentils
½ teaspoon ground cumin	1 tablespoon barley

1. Brown the lamb on all sides in the oil in a small skillet and transfer it to a casserole.
2. In the skillet, sauté the garlic and onion until it is translucent and add all the seasonings. Stir and add to the casserole.
3. Add the water to the skillet and stir to remove all clinging particles. Add this liquid to the casserole.
4. Put the casserole on top of the stove, bring to a boil, cover and place over a flame tamer and simmer ½ hour.
5. Now add the lentils and barley, cover, and let cook at very low heat 1 or 2 hours. Add more water if necessary.

Note: Save any extra lentils for a vegetable serving tomorrow or discard if you are watching your weight.

LAMB CURRY

2 teaspoons vegetable oil
1 small onion, chopped
1 garlic clove, chopped
1 teaspoon curry powder
1 pinch paprika
1 pinch ginger

1 pinch sugar
1 pinch turmeric
¼ teaspoon chili powder
¼ pound lamb, in cubes
2 teaspoons tomato paste
   Beef broth or water

1. Heat the oil in a small casserole and sauté the onion and garlic to golden brown.
2. Stir in the curry powder, paprika, ginger, sugar, turmeric, and chili powder. Sauté until well browned.
3. Add the lamb cubes and brown well. Add the tomato paste, stir, and add broth or water to cover. Simmer 30 minutes or until the lamb is tender. Serve with rice.

LAMB STEW

1 pound lamb neck, cut in 1-inch cubes
1 tablespoon vegetable oil
1 teaspoon flour
½ teaspoon sugar
1 onion, sliced

2 tablespoons sliced green pepper
   Salt and pepper
1 8½-ounce can mixed vegetables
2 small new potatoes, peeled

1. In a small skillet brown the lamb on all sides in the oil.
2. Remove meat to a small casserole, add flour and sugar, and stir.
3. Add onion and green pepper to the skillet, and season with the salt and pepper. Cook, stirring, for 1 or 2 minutes until the onion becomes translucent but not browned.
4. Add vegetables and liquid in the can to the skillet and stir to absorb any brown particles.

5. Pour content of the skillet over the meat in the casserole, bring to a boil, and cover. Cook either on top of the stove over a flame tamer or in a low oven (300 degrees) for 1 hour or until the lamb is tender and potatoes are done.

Note: This recipe makes a double portion. Refrigerate half for another day or invite a friend to dinner.

LAMB AND RICE STEW

1 tablespoon flour	2 tablespoons uncooked rice
Salt and pepper	¾ cup water or chicken broth
1 pound lamb neck and breast with bones, in cubes	1 small potato, halved
	1 carrot, in four pieces
1 tablespoon oil	1 pinch thyme
1 onion, chopped	1 bay leaf
1 garlic clove, minced	

1. Mix the flour, salt, and pepper and place on a sheet of wax paper. Turn the lamb pieces in the mixture to coat all sides.
2. Heat the oil in a skillet and brown the meat on all sides over high heat. Remove the meat to a casserole with a cover.
3. Add the onion and garlic to the skillet and cook several minutes without browning (stirring frequently). Add the rice and stir again.
4. Pour the broth or water into the skillet, stir and scrape the sides, bring to a boil and pour over the meat in the casserole.
5. Add the carrot, potato, thyme, and bay leaf, cover, and simmer about 1 hour or until the rice is cooked and the meat is also tender.
6. Serve the meat and vegetables with a slotted spoon leaving excess liquid in the pan or thicken the liquid with 1 tablespoon of flour shaken with a little water or broth in a small jar with a top.

DILLED LAMB STEW

1 tablespoon flour
Salt and pepper
1 teaspoon dried dill
1 tablespoon corn oil
5½ ounces lean lamb, cut in ½-inch
   cubes (see note)
½ cup chicken broth
3 carrots, cut in ½-inch lengths

¼ cup tomatoes
3 small white onions, peeled
½ garlic clove, cut in half
¼ teaspoon sugar
4 small mushrooms, sliced
2 small potatoes, peeled and
   cubed

1. Mix flour, salt, pepper, and dill on a sheet of wax paper and coat the lamb pieces on all sides.
2. Heat the oil in an ovenproof casserole and sauté the lamb to light brown on all sides.
3. Add all other ingredients, cover, and simmer 1 hour or until the potatoes are done.
4. With a slotted spoon, remove the stew solids and keep warm.
5. Reduce the cooking liquid to ¼ cup by boiling rapidly and thicken to desired consistency with a mixture of flour and water. Pour sauce over the stew and serve.

Note: Lamb cut from the leg is best, but shoulder is often easier to purchase in small quantities.

LAMB STEW FRENCH STYLE

1 tablespoon vegetable oil
5 ounces lean lamb, cut in 1-inch
   cubes
2 tablespoons chopped onion
½ garlic clove, minced
¼ cup beef broth
¼ teaspoon sugar
1 teaspoon flour

Salt and freshly ground black
   pepper
1 medium tomato, peeled, cored
   and diced
1 pinch of thyme
½ bay leaf
2 small potatoes, peeled and cut
   in ½-inch cubes
1 carrot, peeled and cut in ½-inch
   pieces

1. Heat the oil in a small skillet and brown the lamb pieces on all sides. Transfer them to a small casserole.

2. Add the onion and garlic to the skillet and cook stirring a minute or so. Then add the broth and stir to dislodge the clinging brown particles of flavor.
3. To the casserole of lamb add the sugar, flour, salt and pepper and cook stirring a minute or so until well mixed.
4. Add the broth from the skillet to the lamb casserole and follow with the tomato, thyme, and bay leaf. Let the contents boil.
5. Cover the casserole immediately and let it cook on top of the stove over a flame tamer at low heat for 1 hour.
6. Now add the potatoes and carrots and continue cooking until the vegetables are tender to the touch of a fork.
7. Serve over rice with a slotted spoon discarding any excess liquid or reduce the remaining liquid and use a portion for sauce.

Note: If you purchase a small half leg of lamb, bone it and cut it into usable pieces and freeze part for another time or for another dish. Preferably buy a shoulder lamb chop with approximately 5 or so lean ounces showing.

HOTPOT
(Lamb Casserole)

¼ to ½ pound lean lamb, cubed	Salt and freshly ground black
2 small potatoes, thinly sliced	pepper
1 small onion, thinly sliced	¼ teaspoon rosemary, pulverized
1 rib celery, diced	¼ cup beef gravy
1 carrot, thinly sliced	

1. Preheat the oven to 325 degrees.
2. In a casserole with cover layer the vegetables and the lamb in three layers; lamb in the center. Salt and pepper each layer.
3. Mix the rosemary and beef gravy and pour over the casserole.
4. Add enough water to almost cover the ingredients.
5. Bring to a boil on top of the stove, then cover and bake in the oven for 2 hours.
6. Uncover and continue the baking 30 minutes. Check the liquid and add more water if necessary to prevent burning.

LAMB AND EGGPLANT CASSEROLE

5 ounces lean ground lamb	¼ teaspoon salt or to taste
1 cup eggplant, finely chopped	1 pinch paprika
2 tablespoons chopped onion	¼ cup chopped tomatoes
2 teaspoons chopped parsley	1 teaspoon butter

1. Mix well all ingredients except the butter.
2. Melt the butter in a small casserole and coat the bottom and sides.
3. Pour the ingredients into the buttered casserole and cook at 350 degrees for ¾ hour.

CURRIED LAMB WITH LENTILS

1 teaspoon of vegetable oil	Salt and pepper to taste
¼ pound lamb, cubed	⅓ cup vermouth or white wine
¼ garlic clove, crushed	1 tablespoon lentils
1 tablespoon chopped onion	1 teaspoon barley
½ teaspoon each curry powder, turmeric, and cumin	⅓ cup water
	¼ teaspoon tomato paste

1. Heat the oil in a skillet and quickly brown the lamb cubes.
2. Transfer the lamb to a small casserole with cover.
3. Lower the heat and fry the garlic and onion in the skillet for a few minutes until they are translucent.
4. Now add the curry powder, cumin, turmeric, salt and pepper and cook a few minutes, stirring.
5. Transfer the seasonings to the casserole. Deglaze the skillet by adding the vermouth or white wine and scraping the bottom and sides of the pan to remove the tasty particles. Pour the liquid and dissolved particles into the casserole.
6. Add the lentils, barley, water, and tomato paste. Simmer until the lentils and barley are tender, about ¾ hour.

Pork

Ham Steak Simmered with Pineapple
Country-Cured Ham Steak Creole
Ham Steak with Eggplant, Zucchini, and Tomatoes
Ham Steak in Peach Sauce • Ham Baked in Milk
Ham-Vegetable Casserole • Ham with Vegetables and Rice
Braised Pork Loin with Kraut • Braised Pork in Applesauce
Pork and Prunes • Roast Pork Chop
Oven-Barbecued Pork Chops • Braised Pork Chop and Turnip
Pork Chop Braised with Green Pepper
Vinegar Pork Chop Casserole • Pork Chop and Baked Beans
Pork Chop, Baked Beans, and Tomatoes
Braised Stuffed Pork Chop • Deviled Pork Chops
Pork Chops Sauce Piquante • Pork Chops and Green Pepper
Baked Pork Chops with Rice • Mustard Fillet of Pork
Baked Pork and Vegetables • Pork Chop Casserole

The subject of pork always brings memories of slaughter day in my hometown. In the suburbs where we lived several neighbors annually got together and helped out on that day. It was a fascinating day for a small child; all my friends in the neighborhood, boys and tom-boys came over and watched the slaughter of our own purchased hog. There were so many things going on that day. The kill and then the cutting up of the animal into hams, shoulders, sides of bacon, etc. The processes of sausage-making by my mother and helpers. Even the watching of the great kettle in which soap was made out of certain unwanted fat. It was a good lesson in conservation and it was always a festive occasion.

It was a long day, starting very early in the morning. But there was so much bustle and so many people around that I didn't mind. I looked forward to the day when the same happenings took place at the next neighbor's house. There again all the able-bodied men in the neighborhood would assemble accompanied by the gallery of children. Such meetings were scheduled after the first frost and were preliminary to the winter's good eating.

From the produce of this activity came my first meeting with pork. I still find very good pork selections in the market today and I recommend a few good recipes for simple pork dishes.

HAM STEAK SIMMERED WITH PINEAPPLE

⅛ teaspoon oil
¼ pound slice smoked ham, ¼-inch thick approximately

2 slices pineapple
2 tablespoons brown sugar
2 tablespoons pineapple juice

1. Trim the fat edges off the ham slice.
2. Heat the oil in a skillet and sear the ham on both sides. Do this quickly and do not burn the ham. The small amount of oil will help.
3. Cover the ham with the pineapple slices and brown sugar. Add the juice, cover and simmer on top of the stove over low heat and using a flame tamer between the heat and the skillet (optional, but recommended).
4. Simmer until the ham is tender and well cooked, about 50 minutes. Serve hot with the pineapple and juice on top.

COUNTRY-CURED HAM STEAK CREOLE

¼ cup each chopped onion, green pepper, and celery
½ cup canned tomatoes
A pinch of thyme
Salt and pepper

¼ teaspoon chopped parsley
⅛ teaspoon chopped garlic
1 tablespoon butter
1 slice country cured ham

1. Place all ingredients except the ham in a small casserole and cook uncovered on top of the stove for 20 minutes. Cover and place over a flame tamer to keep warm.
2. Make slits in the fat of the ham all around to prevent curling and fry for about 5 minutes on each side. Do not cook dry.
3. Remove the bone from the ham and trim all fat from the sides of the slice.
4. Place the ham on a warm platter and pour the creole sauce into the aperture where the bone was and let it overflow on the ham as it pleases. Serve immediately on a very warm platter.

HAM STEAK WITH EGGPLANT, ZUCCHINI, AND TOMATOES

1 ham steak (preferably country ham) ¼-inch thick
1 small eggplant, thinly sliced
1 small zucchini, thinly sliced
1 medium tomato, thinly sliced
Salt and freshly ground black pepper

1. Place the ham steak in a casserole with cover and cook over moderate heat for 3 minutes.
2. Turn the ham and add the vegetables in layers in the above order. Add pepper and a little salt if it is not country ham, cover and place over a flame tamer.
3. Simmer 50 minutes or until tender.
4. Serve without juice, adding pepper if desired.

HAM STEAK IN PEACH SAUCE

4 ounces trimmed and boned ham steak (preferably country cured ham)
1 teaspoon butter
1 firm peach, defuzzed, pitted, and sliced
Pepper
1 tablespoon lemon juice
1 teaspoon sugar

1. Place the ham in a skillet and add water to cover. Bring to a boil and simmer 3 minutes. Drain. (If the ham is not country cured and salty, omit this process.)
2. Melt the butter in a small skillet and sauté the sliced peach for 1 minute stirring and turning.
3. After draining the ham, let it cook slowly on one side for about 1 minute.
4. Turn the ham, add pepper, and top it with the peaches and the lemon juice mixed well with the sugar.
5. Cover the skillet with aluminum foil and simmer 10 minutes.

HAM BAKED IN MILK

4 ounces trimmed and boned
  ham steak, preferably country
  cured ham
  Oil to grease the baking dish
1 medium potato, sliced

¼ teaspoon dry mustard
½ teaspoon flour
1 tablespoon chopped onion
½ cup milk

1. If you use country ham, parboil it for several minutes to remove excess salt, and drain.
2. Lightly grease the baking dish or casserole. Move the slice of ham about in the oil and turn it over and repeat the motion.
3. Place the potato slices on top of the ham.
4. Mix well the mustard, flour, onion, and milk and pour over the ham and potatoes.
5. Bake covered in a 375 degree oven for 45 minutes; uncover and continue cooking another 15 minutes.

HAM-VEGETABLE CASSEROLE

2 ounces ham (preferably
  country cured; parboiled and
  dried)
1 medium or 2 small potatoes
  (about 3 ounces), sliced
½ medium carrot (about 2
  ounces), sliced

1 small onion (about 1 ounce),
  sliced
½ zucchini (about 3 ounces),
  sliced
1 small tomato (about 5 ounces),
  sliced
  Salt and pepper

1. Layer in a small casserole the ham, then potatoes, carrot, onion, zucchini, and top with tomatoes. Salt and pepper each layer.
2. Cover tightly and place over a flame tamer and low heat. Cook about 50 minutes and serve.

HAM WITH VEGETABLES AND RICE

1 teaspoon butter
2 tablespoons chopped onion
½ garlic clove, finely chopped
1 small zucchini, thinly sliced
5 small mushrooms, sliced
½ cup green beans in ¼-inch lengths
½ cup fresh corn kernels

Salt and pepper
¼ teaspoon oregano
¼ teaspoon parsley, chopped
½ cup canned tomatoes, or sliced cherry tomatoes
½ cup diced cooked ham
½ cup cooked rice

1. Melt the butter in a small casserole and sauté the onion and garlic for 2 minutes or until golden.
2. Add the zucchini, stir, and cook about 5 minutes.
3. Add the mushrooms, beans, corn, and seasonings. Cook 2 minutes.
4. Add the remainder of the ingredients, cover, and simmer ½ hour over very low heat.

BRAISED PORK LOIN WITH KRAUT

2 carrots, sliced
1 onion, sliced
1 garlic clove, minced
1 cup dry sherry (white wine or vermouth may be used)
2 pork chops or a similar portion of loin

Salt and pepper
⅛ teaspoon thyme
1 can sauerkraut, about 8 ounces
½ teaspoon celery seeds
½ tart apple, peeled and sliced

1. Preheat the oven to 450 degrees.
2. In a small casserole, layer the carrots, onion and garlic. Add a splash of the sherry or wine.
3. Season the pork chops with salt, pepper, and thyme and place on top of the vegetables in the casserole.
4. Bake the casserole 20 minutes uncovered. Reduce the heat to 350 degrees.

5. Remove the chops and layer half the sauerkraut mixed with the celery salt and sliced apple into the casserole. Mix well.
6. Now return the chops and place the remainder of the kraut on top of them. Add the remaining sherry and cover. Bake 2 hours or until the chops are well done.
7. If there is too much liquid remaining in the casserole, you may reduce by boiling on top of the stove or just ignore and remove the food with a slotted spoon.

Note: This dish is very good with boiled potatoes and mustard.

BRAISED PORK IN APPLESAUCE

¼ to ½ pound pork loin or trim the bone off a chop or two

Salt and freshly ground black pepper
¼ cup applesauce

1. Trim any excess fat off the pork and season well.
2. Place the pork in a small casserole or other vessel with a tight fitting cover. Spread the pork with applesauce to cover.
3. Place the casserole over low heat using a flame tamer to be sure the pork doesn't burn. Cook covered 2 hours. (You can use the oven if you prefer.)
4. Serve the cooked pork without sauce in which it has cooked. Serve applesauce on the side. Sherry kraut is a good accompaniment.

PORK AND PRUNES

6 prunes, dry or canned
1 or 2 pork chops or loin of pork of similar size

Salt and pepper

1. Soak the dry prunes or dry the canned prunes and remove the pits.
2. With a sharp knife make a pocket in the pork to receive the prunes. Use three prunes for each chop and tie the chop with string in two places so that the prunes say inside during the cooking. Similarly for a loin piece of pork.
3. Preheat the oven to 325 degrees.
4. Salt and pepper the pork and place on a rack in an ovenproof vessel. Bake 2 hours.
5. Drain the fat from the pan and add a little water and stir to loosen the flavorful particles that have derived from the cooking. Serve pan juices over the pork.

ROAST PORK CHOP

Salt and pepper
¼ teaspoon thyme
1 pinch nutmeg (or several passes on the grater)
1 pork chop, about ½ pound
1 white onion, sliced

1 carrot, sliced (and/or one turnip sliced)
4 small mushrooms, sliced
¼ cup vermouth or white wine
¼ cup beef broth

1. Sprinkle the salt, pepper, thyme, and nutmeg on a sheet of wax paper and mix well.
2. Coat the chop in the seasonings by turning it over several times on the wax paper rubbing in the mixture gently.
3. Place the sliced vegetables in a small casserole and lay the seasoned chop on top.
4. Pour over the vermouth or white wine and the beef broth.
5. Roast in the oven at 500 degrees until browned (about 20 minutes). Turn the heat down to 350 degrees and cook covered for 1½ hours.
6. Pour off all the accumulated fat from the casserole (or empty the casserole into a sieve and let the fat drain well). Dampen the chop and vegetables with a dash of broth (1 tablespoon or

so), cover and keep warm until serving time. Top the chop with vegetables.

Note: Instead of serving the chop topped with the cooked vegetables, you may prefer to puree the vegetables by passing them through a sieve or food mill adding any broth necessary to make a sauce of pleasant consistency. Then serve this sauce over the chop.

OVEN-BARBECUED PORK CHOPS

1 or 2 pork chops according to size and appetite	1 tablespoon lemon juice
Salt and pepper	¼ teaspoon worcestershire sauce
¼ cup ketchup	¼ teaspoon Tabasco
	1 tablespoon honey

1. Preheat the oven to 350 degrees.
2. Place chops, well salted and peppered, on a rack in a suitable skillet and bake uncovered for 1 hour.
3. Mix well other ingredients and spread half the mixture on top of the chops. Continue cooking ½ hour.
4. Turn the chops and spread again with the sauce. Cook another ½ hour and serve.

BRAISED PORK CHOP AND TURNIP

1 medium thick pork chop	Salt and pepper
1 onion, sliced	¼ teaspoon thyme
1 carrot, sliced	1 tablespoon sherry
1 turnip, sliced	

1. Trim some fat off chop; slash remaining fat edges.
2. Fry parings in a small skillet and when grease forms, brown chops and onion.
3. Place browned chops and onion in a small casserole and cover with sliced carrot, turnip, salt and pepper.
4. Add sherry and thyme to skillet and stir to dissolve any brown particles. Pour over chop.
5. Cover and cook slowly over a flame tamer for 1 hour. Turn off flame. Reheat when you are ready to serve.

Note: This recipe may be doubled for a guest (except thyme) or double anyway and refrigerate half for another meal.

PORK CHOP BRAISED WITH GREEN PEPPER

Oil or butter to lightly grease the skillet
2 tablespoons vermouth or white wine

1 pork chop trimmed of excess fat
½ cup green pepper, chopped
Salt and pepper

1. Grease the skillet as suggested above to ease the browning of the chop. Place the chop in the skillet and turn to brown on both sides. Remove the browned chop to a small covered casserole and keep warm.
2. Pour the vermouth or white wine into the skillet and add the green pepper. Stir to absorb the pan clingings.
3. Pour the contents of the skillet over the chop in the casserole, season with salt and pepper, cover and simmer or braise until the chop is well done, about 1 hour depending on the thickness of the chop.

VINEGAR-PORK CHOP CASSEROLE

1 large pork chop, or 2 smaller ones	Salt and pepper
1 small onion, chopped	¼ teaspoon thyme
¼ cup wine vinegar	1 carrot, sliced
	1 small turnip, sliced

1. Trim all fat from the chop or chops, render, and discard.
2. Add chopped onion to fat in the pan and cook 2 minutes.
3. Add the vinegar to the pan and scrape the bottom to dissolve the particles that cling.
4. Salt and pepper the chop or chops and place in a small casserole; sprinkle with thyme. Pour over all the vinegar and onion sauce from the skillet. Simmer 1 hour covered on top of the stove using a flame tamer or very low heat.
5. Add sliced carrot and turnip and continue cooking until the vegetables are tender.
6. Serve the meat smothered in vegetables and moistened with 1 tablespoon or so of the liquid remaining. If considerably more liquid remains, reduce it over high heat before using it as a sauce.

PORK CHOP AND BAKED BEANS

1 or 2 pork chops	1 slice onion
1 8-ounce can baked beans	1 slice lemon
1 tablespoon Dijon or Dusseldorf mustard	Freshly ground black pepper

1. Trim most of the fat from the sides of the chop or chops.
2. Place the baked beans in a small casserole or other suitable cooking pan with lid.
3. Spread the mustard over the chop or chops and add to the casserole.

4. Place the onion slice and then the lemon slice on the chop.
5. Sprinkle well with pepper and bake covered at 400 degrees for 40 minutes. Remove the cover for the last 10 minutes.

Note: Serve with additional lemon juice if desired.

PORK CHOP, BAKED BEANS, AND TOMATOES

1 pork chop, trimmed
1 small onion, chopped
1 8-ounce can baked beans

¼ cup canned tomatoes, chopped
1 teaspoon dried basil
   Salt and pepper

1. Salt the bottom of a small skillet and brown the chop on both sides over moderate heat. Shake the skillet and move the chop from time to time to prevent sticking. Remove the chop to a small casserole.
2. Add the onions, beans, tomatoes, and seasonings to the skillet. Bring to a boil. Stir and add to the casserole.
3. Cover the casserole and place it over a flame tamer on top of the stove over low heat. Cook until the chop is well done, about 1 hour.

BRAISED STUFFED PORK CHOP

1 pork chop (about ½ pound)
½ teaspoon butter
¼ cup mushrooms, minced
1 shallot, minced

1 teaspoon rice (or two
   tablespoons bread crumbs)
   Salt and pepper
1 ounce vermouth or white wine

1. Trim the pork chop of all excess fat around the sides and make a slot in the meaty side. The slot should extend to the bone and be as large as you can make it without cutting through the sides. The larger this pocket the easier it is to stuff and secure the stuffing for the cooking.
2. Melt the butter in a skillet and sauté the minced shallot and mushrooms for a minute or so. Do not brown. Add the rice and cook another minute or so. Cool.
3. Stuff the mushroom-shallot mixture into the pocket you have prepared in the chop. Close the opening with the fingers and secure with toothpick. As a safeguard tie a string around the stuffed chop. Wrap it several times around passing the two ends of the opening as well as the center. Alternatively sew the opening closed with needle and string.
4. Brown the chop on both sides in a skillet and transfer it to a small casserole. Salt and pepper the chop and pour the vermouth or wine over all. Cover and simmer 1 hour. Serve hot with a few drops of the liquid in the casserole.

DEVILED PORK CHOPS

1 or 2 pork chops according to size	1 teaspoon worcestershire sauce
1 tablespoon chili sauce	⅛ teaspoon curry powder
1 teaspoon lemon juice	Salt
2 teaspoons minced onion	⅛ teaspoon paprika
⅛ teaspoon dry mustard	¼ cup water
	2 teaspoons olive oil

1. Marinate the chops in a mixture of all ingredients and half the oil for at least 1 hour.
2. Remove and drain the chop or chops. Retain the marinade.
3. Brown the chops in the remaining oil on both sides.
4. Bring the marinade to a boil and pour over the chop or chops. Cover and cook ½ hour in the oven at 400 degrees. Serve with the sauce.

PORK CHOPS-SAUCE PIQUANTE

1 teaspoon butter	¼ teaspoon chopped parsley
2 small pork chops, trimmed	¼ teaspoon tarragon
1 teaspoon chopped shallots	Salt and pepper
4 tablespoons vinegar	2 tablespoons chopped sweet or
½ cup canned tomatoes	sour pickles

1. Melt the butter in a skillet. Add the chops and cook slowly, turning and shaking from time to time to prevent sticking. Cook until the fork inserted in the flesh produces no pink flow of juice. The chops should be well cooked and slowly.
2. Remove the chops to a small casserole and keep warm.
3. To the skillet add the shallots and cook stirring for a minute or so; add the vinegar and deglaze by stirring all the brown particles into the liquid.
4. Add the tomatoes and continue stirring. Add parsley, tarragon, and salt and pepper to taste. Stir again.
5. Pour the sauce over the chops and keep warm or simmer until really well done.
6. Add the chopped pickles, bring to a boil and serve hot.

Note: Boiled carrots are an excellent accompaniment. You can use the chop sauce instead of butter with the carrots.

PORK CHOP AND GREEN PEPPER

1 pork chop, trimmed (about 5 ounces)	¼ teaspoon each sage, thyme, and parsley
Salt and pepper	½ cup canned tomatoes or about
⅓ cup chopped green pepper	the same amount of fresh
⅛ cup chopped onion	tomatoes if you can find good
½ garlic clove, minced	ones

1. Salt and pepper the chop and brown on both sides in a skillet without grease. Just stir to keep from sticking.
2. Remove the chop to a small casserole with cover.
3. Add the peppers, onion, garlic, and herbs to the skillet and cook stirring for 2 minutes. Add the tomatoes last and cook for 1 minute. Stir well.
4. Pour the vegetables over the chop and cover tightly.
5. Simmer over a flame tamer until the chop is tender and well done. About 1 hour according to the thickness of the pork.

BAKED PORK CHOPS WITH RICE

1 pork chop, trimmed	¼ teaspoon oregano
1 tablespoon chopped onion	½ cup canned tomatoes
¼ cup dry rice	½ cup chicken broth
¼ teaspoon sage	Salt and freshly ground pepper
¼ teaspoon thyme	1 teaspoon chopped parsley

1. Dice the fat cut from the rim of the chop and render it in a small casserole. Discard the fat bits and all but 1 teaspoon or so of the rendered grease.
2. Salt and pepper the chop, brown in the pork grease on both sides and remove it from the casserole.
3. Add the onion to the casserole and cook stirring for 1 minute.
4. Combine the dry rice, sage, thyme, and oregano and add to the casserole. Stir well.
5. Now add the tomatoes, chicken broth, and pork chop. Cover and bake at 350 degrees for 1 hour.
6. Serve with parsley to garnish.

MUSTARD FILLET OF PORK

1 teaspoon bacon drippings or butter
½ garlic clove, minced
1 teaspoon dry mustard
Salt and freshly ground black pepper
1 pork chop or two small ones trimmed of almost all fat and bone (about 4 ounces trimmed)

¼ cup dry white wine or vermouth
1 tablespoon minced onion
1 tablespoon minced green pepper

1. Heat the bacon drippings and cook the garlic, stirring, for 1 minute or so.
2. Mix the mustard, salt, and pepper and coat the pork on all sides.
3. Add the pork to the hot drippings and garlic and brown on both sides.
4. Pour in the wine or vermouth and cook until the liquid is reduced by half or to about 2 tablespoons.
5. Add the onion and green pepper, cover, and cook over low heat for 1 hour or until the pork is tender.
6. Remove the pork to a warm platter. If the sauce is too thin, reduce to 1 tablespoon or so by boiling and serve over the pork. Serve with rice or cornbread.

BAKED PORK AND VEGETABLES

5 ounces of pork (1 or 2 chops trimmed of bone and fat)
Salt and freshly ground black pepper
1 tablespoon flour
1 small turnip, cubed (about 3 ounces)

1 small potato, cubed (about 3 ounces)
1 carrot, coarsely sliced (about 3 ounces)
2 tablespoons water
1 teaspoon chopped parsley

1. Season the pork fillets on both sides and place in a small casserole or covered skillet, and place in a 400 degree oven for 20 minutes.
2. Sprinkle with the flour, turn and stir. Continue the cooking for another 20 minutes.
3. Add the vegetables and the water and cook another 20 minutes.
4. Turn, stir, cover and cook 30 minutes longer or thereabouts.
5. Serve on a warm platter. If brown particles are sticking to the sides and bottom of the pan, add a little water to the pan and dissolve the delicious residue and pour it over the dish. Garnish with chopped parsley.

PORK CHOP CASSEROLE

1	large or two small pork chops, trimmed	½	small green pepper, sliced
2	tablespoons raw rice	½	cup canned tomatoes
1	small onion, sliced		Salt and pepper
		¼	cup hot water

1. Place the pork chop or chops in a small casserole with cover.
2. Cover with rice, onion, green pepper, tomatoes, salt, pepper and hot water.
3. Cover and bake at 350 degrees for 1 hour or until well done.

Chicken

Fried Chicken • Stewed Chicken and Vegetables
Boiled Chicken • Poached Chicken with Lemon
Poached Chicken Breast with Leeks
Poached Chicken in Tomato Sauce
Poached Chicken with Mushrooms and Lime Juice
Chicken Sauté • Chicken Sauté in Tomato Sauce
Chicken Breast Sauté with Tomato and Tarragon
Chicken Sauté New Jersey • Chicken with Tomatoes and Cream
Chicken Sauté Chasseur • Country-Style Chicken Sauté
Creamed Chicken • Chicken Creamed with Pimiento
Creamed Chicken with Onion
Breast of Chicken with Cream Sauce
Chicken Breast with Tomatoes and Onions
Chicken with Mushrooms and White Onions in Wine
Chicken Breast with Peas • Stuffed Breast of Chicken
Breast of Chicken Baked with Potatoes
Breast of Chicken Baked with Grapefruit Juice
Vinegar Chicken • Breast of Chicken Parmesan
Mary Chicken • Breast of Chicken Marsala
Chicken Marsala with Shallots and Tomatoes
Chicken Breast in Port
Chicken Breast with Green Pepper and Onion
Smothered Breast of Chicken • Stewed Chicken and Cream Sauce
Deviled Chicken Breast • Deviled Chicken with Ham
Sweet and Sour Baked Chicken • Chicken Creole
Chicken in Peach Sauce • Chicken Cacciatore
Chicken Marengo • Chicken with Olives and Tomato Sauce
Chicken Breast Jersey • Spanish Chicken and Rice
Breast of Chicken, Brown Sauce, and Mushrooms • Chicken Curry

Curried Chicken with Peas • Chicken with Lemon
Chicken in Tarragon Sauce • Mexican-Style Chicken
Chicken Breast Tonnato • Chicken Breast Tetrazzini
Chicken in Tarragon-Wine-Cream Sauce
Breast of Chicken with Carrots
Curried Chicken Wings • Blanquette of Chicken Wings
Chicken Salad • Creamed Chicken and Ham • Chicken à la King

As a boy chicken didn't much appeal to me. Chickens were just too available out there in the back lot and also they seemed to be friends. They always were when I brought the grain. But, as an adult, I have cooked more chicken than anything else because it is not difficult to find good quality chicken and because it is so versatile. Rather bland in itself, chicken is easily brought to a peak of flavor by the addition of seasonings and sauces. And, of course, the price has been comparatively right in recent years.

That reminds me of my aunt's custom of buying a dozen chickens from the farmer's wagon and having them delivered to her chicken coop. The houseboy would wring a neck or two as required. The feature I remember best is that she paid $1.50 for the dozen chickens. (That was in the early decades of the twentieth century.) Don't let that price discourage you now. Chicken is still a good buy.

Chicken has been a feature of many dishes prepared in my kitchen in recent years, but I have come to prefer plain poached chicken with sauce (pages 119-121). It is good with a simple sauce of reduced cooking liquid or with a flavored sauce using lemon or lime, egg yolk and cream, and endless variations are possible. I prefer chicken breast to other parts of the bird, and I like to purchase breast including the rib bones. They add flavor and can be easily removed at serving time if desired. In any of the recipes that follow you may substitute your preference of chicken cuts, either with the bone or boneless.

How to Bone a Chicken Breast

My advice is to keep cool and only bear in mind the objective: to release the chicken flesh from bones. Do not fear the chore as an ordeal. Be bold and just do it. Technique is somewhat unimportant, at least at first. You will improve with practice.

A few pointers to start you off: Use a sharp paring knife and cut the whole breast in half (enough for one serving). Hold one half breast skin down in the left palm if you are right-handed. Thread the knife under the thin small breast bone near its base and cut outward to completely free this bone. Hold the half breast by this liberated bone and slice, whittle or shave downward toward the larger bones along the inside of the ribs. Break off the ribs and discard or put them in the pot for broth. Now there are several larger bones to remove by the most convenient action you choose. Just attack by scraping, sliding, twisting or however you find works best to do the job. When the large bones are free, check the boned breast for slivers and the half of the wishbone. These will slide out easily by pressure from the fingers when the other end of the bone is firm against a cutting board.

These words of "how to" are just one way to start boning a chicken breast, not the only and maybe not the best way. Do it your own way, but do it and have no fear. A boned breast of chicken will reward you for your effort in elegance and you can cut it and eat it with such grace.

FRIED CHICKEN

½ chicken breast or one or two of your favorite chicken pieces
Milk (for a variation try buttermilk sometime)

1 tablespoon flour
Salt and pepper
¾ cup shortening or vegetable oil and butter

1. Place the chicken in a small bowl and add milk to cover. Let stand for at least 1 hour.
2. Remove the chicken from the milk bath onto a paper towel and dry away some of the excess milk.
3. Dredge the chicken on all sides with a flour, salt and pepper mixture.
4. Heat the shortening and add the chicken. Turn once and reduce the heat. Cook for ½ hour turning to brown on both sides.

Note: If you like chicken gravy and can stand the calories, drain off the oil and mix a tablespoon of flour with what remains in the skillet. Cook a minute or so and stir in about ¾ cup of milk or half-and-half. Blend well and test for seasoning. It will need salt.

STEWED CHICKEN AND VEGETABLES

½ chicken breast or a serving of your favorite chicken piece or pieces
1 cup yellow squash, sliced
1 cup tomatoes, diced
½ cup onion, diced

½ cup potatoes, diced
Salt and pepper
¼ teaspoon thyme
1 bay leaf
1 can chicken broth (13¼ ounces or so) or water

1. Place all ingredients in a covered saucepan, bring to a boil and simmer 45 minutes allowing some steam to escape by placing the top of the pan slightly ajar.

2. Remove from the fire and test with a fork for doneness. All ingredients should be tender.
3. Allow the stew to cool in the liquid.
4. At serving time, remove the chicken and vegetables to another pan and rapidly boil 1 cup of the liquid to reduce it to about ½ cup or so.
5. Return the chicken and vegetables to the reduced sauce and heat before serving. If you prefer a thicker sauce, stir in a mixture of 1 teaspoon flour and 1 tablespoon water during the final boiling of the liquid for the purpose of reducing the quantity as well as thickening.

BOILED CHICKEN

½ chicken breast or one serving of your favorite piece or pieces of chicken
Chicken broth (canned or freshly made by boiling chicken bones and water) or water

1 onion studed with 2 cloves
2 carrots
1 bay leaf
5 peppercorns
¼ teaspoon thyme
Salt

1. Bring all ingredients to a boil in a saucepan and simmer 45 minutes skimming the foam and scum which rises to the top.
2. Test the chicken and vegetables for doneness and continue cooking as necessary. Let the chicken and vegetables cool in the liquid.

Note: The chicken may be served in various ways, even cold; however a favorite presentation is with a slightly thickened sauce and the vegetables. Use 1 teaspoon each of butter and flour mixed well and stir in ½ cup liquid that has been used in the boiling.

POACHED CHICKEN WITH LEMON

½ chicken breast or your favorite
   piece or two
   Salt and pepper
½ garlic clove, sliced
1 celery rib with leaves, chopped
½ bay leaf
¼ teaspoon thyme

1 slice lemon
   Chicken broth or water
1 tablespoon butter
1 tablespoon flour
1 tablespoon lemon juice
1 egg yolk

1. Place the chicken, salt, pepper, garlic, celery, bay leaf, thyme, and lemon slice in a suitable pan with cover. Add the broth to cover and bring to a boil. Turn the heat to lowest and simmer for 1 hour or until the chicken is tender.
2. Remove the chicken from the broth and keep warm.
3. Melt the butter in a small pan and stir in the flour. Cook 1 minute stirring.
4. Strain ½ cup of the broth in which the chicken was cooked and stir into the butter and flour mixture. Continue stirring until the sauce is smooth and the lumps have dissolved.
5. Mix the lemon juice and egg yolk well.
6. Off the flame mix a little sauce into the lemon and egg mixture and stir into the remainder of the sauce. Cook 1 minute and serve the sauce over the chicken.

POACHED CHICKEN BREAST
WITH LEEKS

½ chicken breast
1 tablespoon chopped onion
2 small leeks, trimmed, washed, and sliced lengthwise (about half a cup)
2 teaspoons butter
½ garlic clove, minced
½ bay leaf

¼ teaspoon thyme
   Salt and pepper
2 teaspoons flour
¼ cup vermouth or dry white wine
1 tablespoon lemon juice
1 egg yolk

1. Soak the chicken in water for 20 minutes.
2. Sauté the onion and leeks in butter for several minutes and add the garlic, bay leaf and thyme, salt and pepper. Stir in the flour.
3. Drain the chicken and place on the vegetables. Add the vermouth or wine and enough water or chicken broth to cover the chicken. Cover and simmer 45 minutes.
4. At serving time, remove the chicken and put it on a warm platter. Add the lemon juice to the sauce.
5. When the sauce is just beginning to simmer again, add a tablespoon or so to an egg yolk in a small bowl and mix well. Add this to the main vessel of sauce and incorporate well. Do not boil.
6. Pour the warm sauce over the chicken and serve with rice.

POACHED CHICKEN IN TOMATO SAUCE

½ chicken breast or your favorite piece or two
2 tablespoons chopped onion
1 garlic clove, minced
⅓ cup chicken broth

⅓ cup tomato sauce
Salt and freshly ground black pepper
½ bay leaf

1. Place all ingredients in a small casserole.
2. Bring to a boil and simmer 30 minutes or until the chicken is tender.
3. Remove the chicken from the pan and boil the sauce rapidly to reduce and thicken to your taste. Correct the seasoning of the sauce by the addition of salt and pepper if desired and serve it over the chicken.

POACHED CHICKEN WITH MUSHROOMS AND LIME JUICE

1 or 2 of your favorite pieces of chicken
½ cup canned chicken broth
   Salt and pepper
1 tablespoon butter

10 small mushrooms, sliced
1 tablespoon flour
1 egg yolk
1 tablespoon lime juice

1. In a covered small casserole poach the chicken in the broth for ¾ hour or until it is tender to the touch of a fork. Remove the chicken to a warm serving plate.
2. In a small skillet melt the butter and sauté the mushrooms for 2 minutes, stirring.
3. Add the flour to the skillet and stir well while pouring in the broth remaining in the casserole. Smooth out any lumps of flour.
4. Mix the egg yolk and lime juice in a cup and add to it a small portion of the hot broth. Stir well and add this to the main portion of sauce. Stir well but do not boil. Pour the sauce over the chicken and serve it hot.

CHICKEN SAUTE

   Salt and pepper
1 serving of chicken
1 tablespoon butter or vegetable oil or half butter and half oil
2 tablespoons diced shallots or scallions (even onion can be used to slightly less delicious effect)

¼ cup dry white wine or vermouth
1 teaspoon flour
¼ cup chicken stock, canned or fresh

1. Season the chicken on all sides.
2. Melt half the butter and oil, if used, in a skillet and brown chicken on all sides.

3. Remove chicken and pour off excess fat in the skillet.
4. Add remaining butter and the shallots or scallions, and cook 2 minutes or so without browning.
5. Add the wine and stir to dissolve any brown particles clinging to the sides of the pan. Continue cooking until the liquid is almost evaporated.
6. Add the flour, stir and pour in the chicken stock and continue stirring until the sauce has begun to thicken.
7. Return chicken to the skillet and cook 15 minutes; turn and cook 20 minutes longer. Serve hot. You may prepare a short time ahead and leave uncovered until ready to serve. Just heat well before eating.

CHICKEN SAUTE IN TOMATO SAUCE

½ chicken breast, boned and cubed	1 teaspoon flour
Salt and pepper	1 tablespoon white wine or vermouth
½ teaspoon vegetable oil	1 teaspoon tomato paste
¼ cup chopped onions	2 tablespoons chicken broth
¼ garlic clove, minced	¼ teaspoon rosemary, pulverized
1 pinch saffron	

1. Preheat the oven to 375 degrees.
2. Salt and pepper the chicken cubes and brown them in the oil.
3. Add the onion, garlic and saffron and cook 1 minute stirring.
4. Now stir in the flour.
5. Add the wine, tomato paste and broth; then the rosemary.
6. Stir, cover, and bake ½ hour. Serve hot.

CHICKEN BREAST SAUTE WITH TOMATO AND TARRAGON

1 tablespoon flour	1 shallot, diced
Salt and pepper	1 small tomato, peeled, seeded and diced
½ chicken breast	¼ teaspoon dried tarragon
1 tablespoon butter	

1. Place a sheet of wax paper on a flat surface and sprinkle the flour and salt and pepper onto it. Mix the flour and seasonings and coat the chicken breast on both sides.
2. Melt the butter in a small casserole and brown the chicken well on both sides and remove it from the pan.
3. Before the chicken cools, add the shallot to the pan and cook without browning; then add the tomatoes and the tarragon.
4. Return the chicken to the casserole, cover and place the casserole on a flame tamer to insure even heat. Turn the flame to low and simmer for 1 hour or until the chicken is tender.
5. Place the chicken on a warm serving plate, turn up the fire and reduce the casserole contents to a sauce by evaporating excess liquid. Pour this sauce over the chicken and serve hot.

CHICKEN SAUTE NEW JERSEY

½ chicken breast or your favorite piece or two
Salt and pepper
1 teaspoon butter
2 chopped shallots
1 teaspoon flour

3 tablespoons dry white wine or vermouth
2 tablespoon heavy cream
¼ teaspoon thyme
1 egg yolk
¼ teaspoon lemon juice
¼ teaspoon chopped parsley

1. Salt and pepper the chicken and sauté it in butter; first on the skin side for 10 minutes and on the other side for 5 minutes. Shake the pan to prevent burning.
2. Add the shallots and sprinkle with flour and cook another minute covered.
3. Pour in the wine, 1 tablespoon heavy cream and the thyme. Cover and cook 25 minutes over low heat.
4. Remove the chicken and keep warm.
5. In a small bowl combine the egg yolk, lemon juice and the remaining cream. Pour the egg mixture over the chicken off the heat and cook 2 minutes.
6. Serve the sauce over the chicken with parsley to garnish.

CHICKEN WITH TOMATOES AND CREAM

2 tablespoons butter
½ chicken breast or your favorite
   piece or two
½ cup sliced mushrooms
½ cup sliced shallots

½ cup canned tomatoes, chopped
¼ teaspoon tarragon
   Salt and pepper
¼ cup vermouth
2 tablespoons heavy cream

1. Melt 1 tablespoon of butter in a skillet and sauté the chicken, skin side down for 10 minutes; turn and cook over medium heat another 10 minutes or until the chicken is tender.
2. Sauté the mushrooms in the remaining butter. Reserve off the fire.
3. Remove the chicken and keep warm. In the skillet sauté the shallots, add the mushrooms, tomatoes, and tarragon and cook stirring for 5 minutes. Season with salt and pepper.
4. Stir in the vermouth and then the cream; heat thoroughly without boiling. Pour over the chicken and serve.

CHICKEN SAUTE CHASSEUR

½ chicken breast or your favorite
   piece or two
   Salt and pepper
1 tablespoon vegetable oil
½ cup sliced mushrooms
¼ cup diced onion

1 teaspoon flour
¼ cup dry vermouth or white
   wine
½ cup canned tomatoes
¼ teaspoon minced parsley

1. Salt and pepper the chicken and brown it in oil in a skillet (10 minutes on each side).
2. Add the mushrooms, cover and cook 10 minutes.
3. Remove the chicken and keep it warm.
4. When ready to serve, add the onion to the skillet and cook stirring 1 minute or so. Stir in the flour.
5. Now add the vermouth or white wine and reduce by half. Then add the tomatoes and cook 5 minutes stirring continually.
6. Serve the sauce over the chicken and garnish with parsley.

COUNTRY-STYLE CHICKEN SAUTE

½ chicken breast, boned
2 teaspoons flour
   Salt and freshly ground black
   pepper

1 tablespoon butter
2 tablespoons heavy cream

1. Skin the chicken breast and place it between two pieces of wax paper. Pound the chicken with a meat pounder or the bottom of a heavy skillet until it is very thin.
2. Coat the chicken lightly with half the flour, and season.
3. Melt the butter in a skillet and sauté the chicken over moderate heat for 5 minutes on each side.
4. Remove the chicken to a warm platter and keep it warm.
5. Add the remaining flour to the skillet and stir. Then add the cream and continue stirring until the sauce is smooth. Pour the sauce over the chicken and serve it hot.

CREAMED CHICKEN

½ chicken breast
1 cup chicken broth
1 tablespoon butter
1 tablespoon flour

   Salt and pepper
⅛ cup heavy cream (2
   tablespoons)
1 teaspoon chopped parsley

1. Cook chicken in the broth until tender. Cool, skin, bone, and cube the chicken.
2. Melt the butter in a saucepan and stir in the flour to make a paste. Add salt and pepper.
3. Gradually add ¼ cup of the broth in which the chicken was cooked and stir rapidly with a wire whisk. If there is more broth than called for here, enrich what there is by boiling it rapidly until reduced to about ¼ cup.
4. Add the cream; stir and add the chicken. Stir again and turn off the heat.
5. Warm the creamed chicken just before serving and spoon it onto a piece of warm toast. Garnish with parlsey.

CHICKEN CREAMED WITH PIMIENTO

½ pound chicken
1 small onion, diced
  Salt and pepper
  Chicken broth
1 tablespoon butter

1 tablespoon flour
½ cup milk (cream if you want it richer)
¼ cup pimiento, minced

1. Place the chicken, onion, salt and pepper in a saucepan and cover with broth (water may be used but broth is more flavorful and the result is more delicious). Bring to a boil and simmer 20 minutes. Cool.
2. Melt the butter in a small casserole and stir in the flour. Cook stirring for 1 minute or so and pour in the milk all at once stirring vigorously. Continue stirring until the sauce begins to thicken.
3. Cut the chicken in bite-size pieces and add it to the sauce with the pimiento. Turn off the heat, cover, and warm up the casserole when ready to dine.

Note: Use part of the cooking broth instead of the milk or cream or instead of a portion of it as a variation of the above.

CREAMED CHICKEN WITH ONION

½ cup chicken broth
½ cup chopped onion
2 teaspoons flour

1 cup cooked chicken, diced
1 egg yolk
  Salt and pepper

1. In ¼ cup of the broth, cook the onion for 2 minutes.
2. Heat the remaining broth to a simmer and stir in the flour. Blend well.
3. Combine the flour-broth mixture and the onion and broth. Stir until smooth and add the chicken. Keep warm.

4. At serving time, blend a little liquid from the chicken mixture with the egg yolk in a small cup. Add the egg yolk mixture to the chicken and stir well. Check seasonings, heat thoroughly and serve.

BREAST OF CHICKEN WITH CREAM SAUCE

½ chicken breast, boned	½ cup chicken broth
½ onion studded with 1 clove	Salt
½ bay leaf	1 tablespoon butter
1 pinch thyme	1 tablespoon flour
4 peppercorns	¼ cup cream
½ celery rib	4 drops lemon juice
½ garlic clove	

1. Place the chicken breast in a sucepan with all ingredients except the butter and flour, lemon juice and cream. Simmer for about 45 minutes. Remove the chicken and keep it warm. Retain the broth.
2. Melt the butter in a saucepan and stir in the flour. Pour in ¼ cup of the chicken broth remaining in the pan in which the chicken was simmered or add canned broth or water. Blend well with a wire whisk before adding the cream. Continue to stir and add lemon juice.
3. Transfer the chicken breast to the sauce, bring to a boil, cover and keep warm until serving time. This goes very well with rice or noodles.

Note: You can make the broth from the bones taken from the breast by boiling them in water with a pinch of salt, and maybe some onion.

CHICKEN BREAST WITH TOMATOES AND ONIONS

½ chicken breast (or your favorite piece or two)
1 tablespoon olive oil
Salt and freshly ground black pepper

½ cup chopped onion
1 garlic clove, minced
¼ cup dry white wine
½ teaspoon rosemary
½ cup chopped tomatoes

1. Sauté the chicken in olive oil over moderate heat until slightly browned, stirring frequently.
2. Add salt, pepper, onion and garlic and continue cooking until the onion is wilted but not browned.
3. Finally add the wine, rosemary, and tomatoes. Cover and cook 20 minutes or until the chicken is fork tender. Keep warm until serving time and serve over rice. (If the sauce is too thin, boil it rapidly after removing the chicken until it is rich and thick enough not to inundate the plate.)

CHICKEN WITH MUSHROOMS AND WHITE ONIONS IN WINE

1 tablespoon butter
½ chicken breast, boned
1 teaspoon brandy (optional)
7 small mushrooms
4 small white onions
1 pinch thyme

¼ cup vermouth or white wine
½ teaspoon parsley, finely chopped
Salt and pepper
1 teaspoon flour
1 tablespoon water

1. Melt the butter and brown the chicken on both sides. Continue cooking for about 5 minutes.
2. Warm the brandy (put it into a jigger and place it over the pilot area of the stove). Pour the warm brandy over the chicken and ignite it.

3. When the flame dies, add the mushrooms, onions, thyme, vermouth, parsley, salt and pepper. Cover tightly and simmer ¾ hour.
4. Remove the chicken and other solids from the casserole and thicken the sauce by stirring in the water and flour mixture (shake vigorously together in a small jar with tight fitting cap).
5. Return the chicken, etc. to the casserole, cover and keep warm until serving time.

CHICKEN BREAST WITH PEAS

½ chicken breast, boned and skinned	¼ teaspoon thyme
2 teaspoons oil	½ cup canned peas
Salt and pepper	¼ cup canned tomatoes, sieved
¼ teaspoon rosemary	1 tablespoon butter
2 tablespoons onion, chopped	¼ teaspoon parsley, finely chopped
¼ cup dry white wine	Grated Parmesan cheese

1. Place the chicken breast between two pieces of wax paper and pound with the bottom of a skillet or other heavy implement.
2. Heat the oil and cook the chicken for 5 minutes turning once.
3. Season with salt and pepper and rosemary.
4. Add the onion, stir.
5. Add the wine and thyme, cover and cook 5 minutes.
6. Keep warm until serving time. Then uncover and turn up the heat to evaporate the wine.
7. Now add the peas, tomatoes, butter and parsley and cover and bake at 375 degrees for 15 minutes.
8. Stir and serve with grated cheese.

STUFFED BREAST OF CHICKEN

½ chicken breast	1 tablespoon chopped celery
Salt and pepper	⅛ teaspoon thyme
2 teaspoons butter	⅛ teaspoon chopped parsley
1 tablespoon chopped onion	⅛ teaspoon basil
1 teaspoon chopped green pepper	1 drop Tabasco
	1 slice dry white bread

1. Wash and dry the chicken breast and place skin side down on a sheet of aluminum foil. Salt and pepper lightly.
2. Melt the butter in a small skillet and sauté the onion, green pepper and celery for 1 minute or so until the onion becomes translucent. Season with thyme, parsley, basil, salt, pepper and Tabasco. Stir well.
3. Crumble the slice of bread in a small bowl with the fingers. Work it to rather fine grains.
4. Now add the sautéed preparation and mix very well, stirring and pressing and stirring again to incorporate the flavors.
5. Press the stuffing against the rib bones of the chicken breast. Press well and fold over the aluminum foil to seal.
6. Place the stuffed package on a small ovenproof utensil or on a small skillet with metal handle (to insure no burning of a wooden one) and bake at 400 degrees for 40 minutes. Open the foil for the last 5 minutes. Test for doneness by piercing with a fork. Serve very hot.

BREAST OF CHICKEN BAKED WITH POTATOES

1 tablespoon olive oil	1 bay leaf
1 garlic clove, minced	½ cup potatoes in ¼-inch dice
½ chicken breast	Salt and freshly ground black pepper
¼ cup dry white wine	
¼ teaspoon rosemary	

1. Heat the oil in a small casserole with cover and sauté the garlic and chicken uncovered until light brown.
2. Add the wine, rosemary, and bay leaf; cover and simmer for about 6 minutes.
3. Add the salt, pepper and potatoes; cover again and bake in the oven for 30 minutes at 350 degrees or until the potatoes are tender. Check liquid from time to time and add a bit more wine or water as needed to prevent burning.
4. Serve with the sauce which may be reduced by boiling rapidly before serving.

BREAST OF CHICKEN BAKED WITH GRAPEFRUIT JUICE

½ chicken breast	Salt and pepper
⅛ teaspoon vegetable oil	⅛ teaspoon tarragon
4 teaspoons grapefruit juice	⅛ teaspoon paprika

1. Place the breast of chicken skin side down in a shallow foil-lined baking dish.
2. Combine the other ingredients and pour over the chicken.
3. Fold the excess foil over the chicken and bake at 400 degrees for 25 minutes.
4. Turn the chicken and leave the foil open. Return to the oven and bake another 25 minutes. Baste from time to time and add water, if necessary. Or reclose the foil to conserve liquid.
5. Serve the chicken on a warm plate and pour over the remaining liquid. If there is no liquid left, add a tablespoon or so of water and mix well to gather as much of the almost caramelized particles as possible. They dilute to a good sauce.

VINEGAR CHICKEN

½ chicken breast
   Flour for dredging
1 tablespoon oil
2 tablespoons onion, minced

3 tablespoons vinegar
¼ teaspoon sugar
   Salt and pepper

1. Dredge the chicken in the flour and brown in oil in a small skillet.
2. Remove the chicken to a small casserole and keep warm.
3. Sauté the onion in the skillet adding a bit more oil or butter if required. Do not burn.
4. When the onion starts to brown slightly add the vinegar and sugar and mix well.
5. Pour the onion-vinegar mixture over the chicken, season with salt and pepper, cover and simmer over a flame tamer on top of the stove or place in a low oven (300 degrees). The cooking will require ½ hour.

BREAST OF CHICKEN PARMESAN

   Flour for dredging
   Salt and pepper
½ chicken breast, boned

½ teaspoon olive oil
¼ cup chicken broth
2 tablespoons Parmesan cheese

1. Mix flour, salt, and pepper on a sheet of wax paper and coat chicken with the mixture.
2. Brown chicken quickly in hot oil.
3. Add broth, sprinkle cheese over chicken and place in a preheated 400 degree oven for 15 minutes.
4. Remove chicken to a warm plate and add seasoned flour to skillet. Stir and add 1 tablespoon of water if necessary to thin sauce.
5. Pour sauce over chicken and serve immediately.

MARY CHICKEN

Salt and pepper   ½ chicken breast
Flour for dredging   ½ strip bacon

1. Mix flour, salt, and pepper on a sheet of wax paper and coat chicken.
2. Place chicken in a frying pan, cover with bacon, add ½ inch of water or chicken broth and bake 1 hour in a 350 degree oven.
3. Remove chicken to a warm serving plate. Pour off pan liquids and stir in ½ tablespoon of flour, add ½ cup liquid (cream, milk, or the defatted pan liquid) and blend scraping brown particles from the pan. Cook, stirring, until sauce attains desired consistency. Correct seasoning to taste. Pour over chicken and serve.

BREAST OF CHICKEN MARSALA

2 tablespoons flour   2 tablespoons butter
  Salt and pepper   4 tablespoons marsala wine
½ chicken breast, boned

1. Place flour, salt, and pepper on a sheet of wax paper and mix well.
2. Coat the chicken with the flour mixture on both sides.
3. Melt the butter in a small skillet and brown the chicken well on both sides.
4. Remove the chicken to a small casserole. Add the marsala wine to the skillet and stir to dissolve the particles clinging to the bottom.
5. Pour the liquid from the skillet over the chicken in the casserole. Cover and place over a small flame on top of the stove. Simmer for ½ hour.
6. Remove the chicken to a warm place and turn up the flame until the liquid is reduced to about 2 tablespoons. Pour this over the chicken and serve hot.

CHICKEN MARSALA WITH SHALLOTS AND TOMATOES

½ chicken breast, boned
Salt and pepper
1 tablespoon butter
1 tablespoon chopped shallots

¼ cup marsala wine
1 cup canned tomatoes, drained and sieved
3 tablespoons chopped parsley

1. Salt and pepper the chicken breast and brown it in butter. Remove the chicken to a casserole with lid.
2. Add the shallots to the skillet in which the chicken was browned. Stir and cook 3 minutes.
3. Add the marsala to the skillet and stir to dissolve the brown particles that cling to the bottom and sides. Simmer 3 minutes and add the tomatoes. Pour the liquid over the chicken and add the parsley.
4. Cover the chicken and simmer 20 minutes.
5. When ready to serve, reheat the casserole and present with rice.

CHICKEN BREAST IN PORT

½ chicken breast, boned and skinned
1 tablespoon flour
¼ teaspoon salt

1 or 2 scrapes of nutmeg
1 tablespoon butter
¼ cup cream
3 tablespoons port wine

1. Place the chicken breast between layers of wax paper and pound with an iron skillet or other device to thin out the flesh.
2. Mix the flour, salt and nutmeg and coat the chicken on both sides.
3. Melt the butter in a skillet and brown the chicken on both sides. Remove the chicken from the pan.
4. Pour the cream into the pan and stir well to dislodge the cooking residue. Add the wine and stir.

5. Return the chicken to the pan, cover and cook 20 minutes.

Note: If the sauce clings to the pan or is too thick, add some milk or cream and stir before pouring over the chicken.

CHICKEN BREAST WITH GREEN PEPPER AND ONION

1 tablespoon butter	½ chicken breast
2 tablespoons onion, chopped	1 teaspoon chopped shallots
1 garlic clove, minced	3 tablespoons dry white wine or vermouth
2 tablespoons chopped green pepper	3 tablespoons chicken broth
4 small mushrooms, chopped	Salt and pepper
¼ cup tomato sauce	

1. Melt half the butter and sauté the onion, garlic, and green pepper for about 2 minutes.
2. Add the mushrooms, stir and cook another minute.
3. Add the tomato sauce and stir again. Let simmer.
4. Brown the chicken in the remaining butter, both sides.
5. Remove the chicken and keep warm.
6. Add shallots to the skillet, stir and add the wine and scrape the sides and bottom of the skillet to dislodge the browned particles.
7. Let the wine almost evaporate and then stir in the chicken stock or broth.
8. Return the chicken to the casserole or covered pan with the sauce, season, and keep warm until serving time.

SMOTHERED BREAST OF CHICKEN

1 tablespoon flour	1 tablespoon butter
Salt and pepper	¼ cup milk
½ chicken breast	

1. Mix the flour, salt and pepper and coat the chicken on all sides.
2. Melt the butter and brown the chicken lightly.
3. Cover the chicken tightly and cook over low heat ¾ hour or until the chicken is tender.
4. Heat the milk to boiling and pour over the chicken, cover and let blend for a few minutes. Serve with the sauce.

Variations: The variations are endless. Of course the chicken breast may be boned for a more elegant appearance. The milk may be eliminated or changed to cream. Additional flour may be added to increase the thickness of the sauce. And the sauce may be flavored with your favorite whim of the moment or at least you can add fresh tomato, tomato purée, curry powder, and almost any flavor available. Other parts of the chicken also taste good when cooked as above.

STEWED CHICKEN AND CREAM SAUCE

½ chicken breast	1 celery rib, trimmed and sliced
1 small onion studded with 1 clove	1 garlic clove, peeled
1 bay leaf	¼ teaspoon salt
¼ teaspoon thyme	1 tablespoon butter
3 peppercorns	1 tablespoon flour
1 carrot, peeled and sliced	¼ cup cream
	Freshly ground black pepper

1. Place the chicken in a pan, add the vegetables, and seasoning, bring to a boil and simmer about 40 minutes until the chicken is tender.

2. Remove the chicken from the pan and keep warm. Turn up the fire and reduce the cooking liquid to about ¼ cup.
3. Melt the butter in a saucepan and stir in the flour. Blend well and pour in the reduced cooking liquid stirring rapidly with a wire whisk. Finally stir in the cream and turn off the fire. Test the seasoning and add salt and pepper to taste.
4. Add the chicken to the sauce and a piece or two of the carrot and celery from the original cooking liquid. When ready to serve, warm the dish but do not boil.

DEVILED CHICKEN BREAST

½ chicken breast	2 teaspoons Dijon mustard
Salt and freshly ground black pepper	¼ teaspoon worcestershire sauce
	⅓ cup chicken broth
1 tablespoon butter	4 tablespoons breadcrumbs

1. Sprinkle the chicken with salt and pepper.
2. Melt the butter in a small casserole and coat the chicken on both sides.
3. Bake the chicken in the oven at 400 degrees for 10 minutes, covered.
4. Turn the chicken and bake the other side another 10 minutes.
5. Shake the mustard, worcestershire sauce, and broth in a small covered jar until well blended.
6. Pour half the mustard mixture over the chicken and bake another 10 minutes, adding half the crumbs.
7. Turn the chicken again, add the remaining crumbs, and mustard sauce and bake another 10 minutes.

DEVILED CHICKEN WITH HAM

½ chicken breast or your favorite piece or pieces	¼ teaspoon worcestershire sauce
	⅓ cup chicken broth
Salt and freshly ground black pepper	1 to 2 ounces bacon or thinly sliced ham or prosciutto, diced
1 tablespoon butter	⅓ scant cup breadcrumbs
2 teaspoons Dijon mustard	

1. Sprinkle the chicken with salt and pepper.
2. Melt the butter in a small casserole and coat the chicken on both sides.
3. Bake the chicken for 10 minutes at 400 degrees.
4. Blend the mustard and worcestershire sauce in half the chicken broth.
5. Fry the bacon or ham for 5 minutes and discard the drippings. Add to the chicken casserole.
6. Turn the chicken and bake another 10 minutes, turn again.
7. Pour the mustard sauce over the chicken and sprinkle with half the breadcrumbs. Bake 10 minutes longer.
8. Turn the chicken and spread the other side with the remaining breadcrumbs. Bake another 10 minutes.
9. Transfer the chicken to a warm serving plate and stir the remaining broth into the cooking pan and serve over the chicken as a sauce.

SWEET AND SOUR BAKED CHICKEN

½ chicken breast	1 tablespoon light brown sugar
1 tablespoon flour	2 tablespoons chopped sweet
Salt and pepper	pickles
2 tablespoons vegetable oil	1 teaspoon worcestershire sauce
2 tablespoons wine vinegar	2 teaspoons ketchup

1. Place flour, salt and pepper in a paper bag and introduce the chicken, washed and dried on paper towels, and shake to coat on all sides.
2. Heat the oil in a small casserole and brown the chicken on both sides.
3. Mix well vinegar, sugar, pickles, worcestershire sauce, and ketchup.
4. Pour the seasonings over the chicken and bake 20 minutes at 350 degrees, covered. Uncover the casserole, baste the chicken with the sauce in the bottom of the casserole and bake another 10 minutes. Serve hot.

CHICKEN CREOLE

½ chicken breast or your favorite piece
1 tablespoon vegetable oil
Salt and freshly ground pepper
2 tablespoons chopped shallots

3 tablespoons chopped green pepper
¼ teaspoon thyme
¼ teaspoon basil
⅓ cup tomato sauce

1. Heat the oil in a skillet and brown the chicken on both sides.
2. Remove the chicken to a small casserole with a top.
3. Add the green peppers and seasonings to the skillet and cook stirring for several minutes.
4. Add the tomato sauce and continue the cooking and stirring another several minutes.
5. Pour the sauce over the chicken, cover and simmer on top of the stove using a flame tamer until the chicken is fork tender (about ½ hour).
6. Serve hot with rice and the sauce.

CHICKEN IN PEACH SAUCE

2 tablespoons butter
½ chicken breast or your favorite piece or two
Salt and pepper
¼ cup water
2 tablespoons minced onion

1 tablespoon (3 teaspoons) lemon juice
1 medium firm peach, pitted and sliced
2 tablespoons sugar
⅛ teaspoon paprika

1. Melt 1 tablespoon of butter in a frying pan. Salt and pepper the chicken and brown it on both sides. Add the water and simmer 20 minutes.
2. Sauté the onion in 2 teaspoons of the butter. Sprinkle it with 2 teaspoons of the lemon juice and let it stand. Do not overcook the onion—a minute or so is enough.
3. In the remaining teaspoon of butter, sauté the peach. Cook to golden.
4. Add the onion, peach, and a mixture of sugar and the remaining

lemon juice to the chicken. Sprinkle with paprika, cover with a lid or aluminum foil, and simmer 20 minutes.
5. Serve hot with the sauce. It is good with rice.

CHICKEN CACCIATORE

1 or 2 of your favorite pieces of chicken	½ garlic clove, minced
1 tablespoon olive oil	½ cup stewed tomatoes
1 medium onion, chopped	¼ teaspoon dried tarragon
2 tablespoons chopped green pepper	Salt and pepper
	¼ cup dry red wine
	7 mushroom caps

1. Soak the chicken in water for ½ hour or so and drain.
2. Heat the oil in a skillet and sauté the chicken to golden on both sides. Transfer to a casserole.
3. Add to the skillet the onion, green pepper, and garlic and cook 5 minutes.
4. Add tomatoes, tarragon, salt and pepper and bring to a boil. Pour over the chicken in the casserole, cover and simmer 20 minutes.
5. Add wine and mushrooms and simmer another 20 minutes.
6. Remove the chicken and mushrooms and reduce the sauce to about ½ cup by boiling rapidly. Serve the sauce over the chicken with rice.

CHICKEN MARENGO

½ chicken breast or your favorite piece or pieces of chicken	1 tablespoon flour
	Salt and pepper

¼ teaspoon tarragon
1 tablespoon olive oil
¼ cup dry white wine or
  vermouth

10 small mushrooms, sliced
¼ cup canned tomatoes, sieved
½ garlic clove, minced
¼ teaspoon parsley

1. Soak the chicken in water to cover for about 30 minutes, drain and dry.
2. Combine the flour, salt, pepper, and tarragon in a bag or on a sheet of wax paper and coat the chicken on all sides. Reserve the flour.
3. Heat the oil in a skillet and brown the chicken over moderate heat on all sides. Transfer to a small casserole.
4. Add the reserved flour mixture to the skillet and stir; add the wine and stir until the mixture is smooth and all the lumps are dissolved. Pour over the chicken in the casserole.
5. Add the mushrooms, drained tomatoes and garlic, cover and bake at 350 degrees for 20 minutes.
6. Uncover the casserole, stir, baste the chicken and recover. Continue the cooking another 20 minutes. Let stand a few minutes before serving. Garnish with parsley.

CHICKEN WITH OLIVES AND TOMATO SAUCE

½ chicken breast or your favorite
  piece or pieces of chicken
1 tablespoon butter
1 tablespoon chopped shallots
½ garlic clove, chopped
  Salt and pepper
3 mushrooms, sliced

1 tablespoon flour
1 tablespoon tomato paste
¼ cup dry white wine
½ cup chicken broth
6 pitted green olives or stuffed
  ones, sliced

1. Melt the butter in a suitable casserole with cover and brown the chicken on all sides. Remove the chicken.
2. Add to the casserole the shallots, garlic, salt and pepper and cook, stirring, for a few minutes.

3. Now add the mushrooms, flour, tomato paste, wine and chicken broth. Stir and cook another minute or so.
4. Return the chicken to the casserole, bring to a boil and cover. Cook at low simmer ½ hour. Add the olives.
5. Remove the chicken to a warm serving plate; turn up the heat in the casserole and reduce the sauce to the desired consistency. I like it thick.

CHICKEN BREAST JERSEY

½ chicken breast	1 teaspoon curry powder
¼ cup white wine or vermouth	½ bay leaf
½ green pepper, chopped	¼ teaspoon thyme
2 small carrots, peeled and diced	1 teaspoon flour
1 small potato, peeled and cut in half	1 teaspoon butter
	1 teaspoon lemon juice
1 small onion, peeled and sliced	¼ cup cream or milk
½ garlic clove, minced	1 egg yolk

1. Soak the chicken in water for about 30 minutes.
2. Place the soaked chicken in a small casserole and add the wine or vermouth, green pepper, carrots, potato, onion, garlic, curry powder, bay leaf, thyme, and water to nearly cover. Bring to a boil.
3. Simmer 50 minutes and add the flour mixed well with the butter. Simmer another minute or so. Keep warm.
4. At serving time stir the lemon juice and cream into the egg yolk and add a little of the liquid from the chicken and vegetable mixture. Stir and add to the casserole. Heat, but do not boil.

SPANISH CHICKEN AND RICE

½ chicken breast or your favorite
  piece or two
2 teaspoons olive oil
1 tablespoon chopped onion
½ garlic clove, minced
2 slices bacon, diced

2 tablespoons uncooked rice
1 small tomato, peeled, cored,
  and chopped
  Salt and pepper
⅛ teaspoon (a pinch) saffron
½ cup chicken broth

1. Brown the chicken well on all sides in the oil.
2. Add the onion, garlic, and bacon. Cook until the onion is wilted.
3. Now add the rice and cook a minute or so. Then add the tomato, salt and pepper, and saffron mixed in the broth.
4. Bring to a boil and simmer ½ hour or until the rice is cooked.

BREAST OF CHICKEN, BROWN SAUCE, AND MUSHROOMS

½ chicken breast
2 teaspoons vegetable oil
1 shallot, chopped
1 celery rib, diced
4 mushrooms, sliced

¼ cup beef gravy
¼ cup water
1 tablespoon tomato paste
  Salt and pepper

1. In a small casserole brown the chicken in oil.
2. Remove the chicken breast and add the chopped shallot and celery to the casserole. Stir and cook a few minutes.
3. Add the mushrooms and continue the cooking another minute or so.
4. Now add the mixture of beef gravy, water and tomato paste well blended.
5. Season the casserole, cover it and simmer on top of the stove over low heat for 1 hour or until the chicken is tender.
6. Thin the sauce with water if it is too thick and serve it hot over the chicken.

CHICKEN CURRY

½ chicken breast or other chicken meat, cooked and diced to make about ½ cup	½ cup curry sauce (see recipe, page 229)

1. Use leftover cold chicken or simmer the breast or other meat in salted water or chicken broth for 10 minutes or until it is tender to the touch of a fork. Skin and dice the flesh.
2. Warm the sauce in a small casserole and add the cooked chicken. Mix well and keep warm until serving time.

Note: Serve with rice and a garnish of chutney.

CURRIED CHICKEN WITH PEAS

1 teaspoon vegetable oil	½ teaspoon cumin
2½ ounces chicken, cubed	Salt and pepper
1 tablespoon chopped onion	½ cup water
¼ garlic clove, minced	1 tablespoon dried peas (split peas)
½ teaspoon curry powder	
¼ teaspoon turmeric	1 teaspoon barley

1. In a skillet heat the oil and brown the chicken over high heat.
2. Transfer the chicken to a small casserole, lower the heat and fry the onion and garlic until the onion is translucent.
3. Now add the curry powder, turmeric, cumin, salt and pepper. Stir well and cook 2 minutes.
4. Place the seasonings in the casserole and deglaze the skillet with the water scraping all brown particles. Add to the casserole.
5. Add the peas and in about 15 minutes the barley. Cook at low heat until the peas and barley are tender, about ¾ hour.

CHICKEN WITH LEMON

1 tablespoon butter	1 tablespoon finely chopped
Salt and pepper	shallots
½ chicken breast	2 tablespoons white wine
	3 thin lemon slices

1. Melt the butter in a suitable casserole. Salt and pepper the chicken breast.
2. Place the breast skin side down in the casserole and brown it well. Turn to let the other side brown.
3. Sprinkle the chopped shallots over the chicken, cover and cook 5 minutes.
4. Pour off the fat and add the wine and lemon slices. Cover again and cook over medium heat 15 minutes or until tender.
5. Serve the chicken with the sauce poured over all. You can let the chicken stand covered while you finish your cocktail and warm at the last minute, but serve hot.

CHICKEN IN TARRAGON SAUCE

½ chicken breast	1 teaspoon flour
¼ cup dry white wine	1 teaspoon butter
¼ cup chicken broth	2 tablespoons milk (or heavy
1 teaspoon dried tarragon	cream if you don't mind the
Salt and pepper	calories)

1. Place the chicken breast in a casserole skin side down and add the wine, broth, tarragon, salt and pepper. Bring to a boil, cover, and cook 20 minutes.
2. Remove the chicken when you are ready to finish the dish. This can wait, but keep the chicken warm. Usually I just turn off the heat and let the chicken rest in the casserole and warm it at the final moment.

3. Turn up the heat and reduce the sauce to about 3 tablespoons.
4. Now mix the flour and butter well and stir it a little at a time into the sauce. When the sauce is thickened to your taste, pour over the chicken and enjoy it.

MEXICAN-STYLE CHICKEN

1 chicken breast or your favorite piece or two	1 teaspoon chili powder
Salt and freshly ground black pepper	¼ teaspoon cumin
	¼ teaspoon oregano
2 teaspoons olive oil	2 teaspoons flour
½ cup finely chopped onion	½ cup chopped tomatoes, fresh or canned Italian plum tomatoes
1 garlic clove, mashed	
1 tablespoon dry sherry	6 pitted green olives

1. Salt and pepper the chicken and brown it in the olive oil skin side down over medium heat; turn and brown the other side. Remove the chicken to a suitable casserole.
2. Add the onion and garlic to the pan in which the chicken was browned, stir, and cook until the onion wilts. Do not burn the onion.
3. Add half the sherry and cook until most of the liquid evaporates.
4. Sprinkle with chili powder, cumin, and oregano. Add the flour. Blend well.
5. Add the tomatoes and cook over low heat about 10 minutes.
6. Pour the sauce over the chicken in the casserole, cover and cook 30 minutes over low heat or until the chicken is tender to the probe of a fork.
7. Add the olives and remaining sherry and bring to a boil and serve hot. Alternately you can delay this last step and reheat at serving time; then add the olives and sherry and bring to a boil.

Note: Half of the chicken breast is ordinarily enough for one serving. The other half will be even better warmed up the next day.

CHICKEN BREAST TONNATO

½ chicken breast
½ can (3½ ounces) tuna in oil
1 small onion, sliced
1 celery rib, diced
½ cup white wine or vermouth or sherry

¼ teaspoon thyme
Salt and pepper
¼ teaspoon sage
¼ teaspoon parsley
1 tablespoon mayonnaise
Several capers

1. Bring to a boil all ingredients except the mayonnaise and capers. Simmer 1 hour. Remove the chicken and cool.
2. Boil and reduce the sauce to about ¼ cup. Strain or put through a food mill.
3. Slice the chicken breast very thinly and arrange on a plate.
4. Blend the mayonnaise and 3 tablespoons of the tuna sauce. Spread the tuna mayonnaise over the sliced chicken, garnish with capers, and refrigerate until serving time.

CHICKEN BREAST TETRAZZINI

½ chicken breast
1 small onion studded with one clove
½ stalk celery
Salt
¼ bay leaf
1 tiny carrot (about one tablespoon in volume)
1 cup chicken broth

1 teaspoon butter
1 teaspoon flour
A dash of Tabasco
1 egg yolk
⅛ pound spaghetti
1 teaspoon dry sherry
3 tablespoons grated Parmesan cheese

1. Place the chicken, onion, celery, salt, bay leaf, carrot and broth in a suitable pot and simmer until tender. It should take about 20 minutes. Test the chicken with a fork. Remove the chicken and let it cool. Remove the skin and bones.
2. In another pan melt the butter and stir in the flour. Now pour

in the remaining broth which should be about ¾ cup. If not reduce by boiling rapidly for a few minutes. Pour the broth in all at once and stir rapidly with a wire whisk. Add the Tabasco. Continue stirring until the sauce is smooth.

3. Put the egg yolk in a small saucer. Add a spoonful or so of the sauce and mix well. Then pour into the main body of sauce and stir well. Turn off the heat.

4. Cook spaghetti according to the package directions. Drain and flush with cold water.

5. In a buttered casserole layer spaghetti, chicken and then the remainder of spaghetti. Pour the sauce over all; add the sherry and the cheese.

6. At serving time place uncovered under the preheated broiler until the cheese is melted and the top of the casserole is brown.

CHICKEN IN TARRAGON-WINE-CREAM SAUCE

2 teaspoons butter
2 teaspoons flour
½ cup chicken broth
1 teaspoon dry tarragon powdered in a mortar and pestle
½ chicken breast or your favorite piece or two

Salt and freshly ground black pepper
1 tablespoon minced shallots
¼ cup dry white wine
3 tablespoons light or heavy cream

1. Melt half the butter in a saucepan, add the flour, stir and add the chicken broth, stir again and cook 2 minutes or so; now add the tarragon and let cook 10 minutes.

2. In a small skillet melt the remaining butter and brown the chicken on both sides. Season with salt and pepper. Cook over reduced heat 15 to 25 minutes or until tender.

3. Remove the chicken from the skillet and keep warm in a small covered casserole over low heat.

4. Add the shallots to the skillet and cook several minutes stirring well. Pour in the wine and scrape the bottom of the skillet to dislodge the clinging particles of flavor. Let the wine boil down to almost zero.
5. Pour in the broth and mix well, cook a minute or so and add the cream; stir well and bring to a boil. Pour over the chicken.
6. Serve the chicken hot with the sauce.

BREAST OF CHICKEN WITH CARROTS

½ chicken breast
2 carrots, peeled and sliced
¼ teaspoon oregano

¼ teaspoon dried thyme
Salt

1. In a metal casserole with tight fitting cover, place the washed chicken breast, skin side down.
2. Top the chicken with carrots and add seasonings. Add water to a depth of ½ inch.
3. Cover the casserole and place over a flame tamer on top of the stove, over low heat.
4. Let the casserole contents cook until the carrots are tender, about 1 hour.
5. Remove with a slotted spoon the chicken and carrots and keep warm.
6. Place the casserole and cooking juices over high heat and reduce to 2 tablespoons or about that.
7. Serve the chicken and carrots on a warm plate and pour the sauce over all.

Note: Instead of reducing the liquids by boiling you may prefer a thickened sauce. Stir in a blend of 1 teaspoon of flour and 3 tablespoons of water shaken well in a small jar with tight fitting top. Or use beurre manie (butter and flour blended together and stirred into the sauce a little at a time until the desired thickness is reached).

CURRIED CHICKEN WINGS

2 tablespoons butter	Salt and pepper
½ medium apple, peeled, cored, and finely diced	1 tablespoon curry powder or to taste
¼ banana, finely chopped	½ cup canned tomatoes
1 tablespoon chopped celery	½ cup chicken broth
2 tablespoons chopped onion	3 chicken wings or ½ chicken breast if you prefer
½ garlic clove, finely chopped	

1. Heat half the butter in a saucepan and add the apple, banana, celery, onion, garlic, salt and pepper. Cook until the onion is translucent stirring frequently.
2. Sprinkle the sauce with curry powder and mix well. Add the tomatoes, then the broth and stir again. Cook over low heat for 40 minutes or so until the vegetables are very tender.
3. Sieve the sauce and cook a minute longer. Keep warm.
4. Snip off the tip of the wing with a chicken shears. Salt and pepper the chicken and brown it on all sides in the remaining butter (3 to 5 minutes on one side and 8 to 10 minutes on the other).
5. Add the chicken to the sauce and keep warm until serving time.
6. Heat well and serve with rice.

Note: If you don't mind the calories, swirl into the sauce another portion of butter before adding the chicken.

BLANQUETTE OF CHICKEN WINGS

4 chicken wings	2 tablespoons flour
1 tablespoon butter	2 shakes powdered dill
½ garlic clove, minced	1 shake nutmeg
2 tablespoons minced onion	1 cup chicken broth

1. Snip off the small tip of the wings and discard.
2. Melt butter in a small casserole, add the chicken wings, garlic and onion and cook 5 minutes stirring to prevent burning.
3. Add the flour, dill and nutmeg and continue stirring for another minute.
4. Pour over all the broth and bring to a boil.
5. Place in a 325-degree oven and cook 1 hour covered.
6. Thicken the liquid if desired and serve hot with rice.

CHICKEN SALAD

½ cup cooked chicken	Salt
¼ cup diced celery	¼ teaspoon paprika
¼ cup (4 tablespoons) mayonnaise	

1. Skin and bone the chicken and cut into ½-inch cubes.
2. Add the celery, mayonnaise, salt and paprika and mix well. Let stand in the refrigerator until serving time.
3. Serve cold on a lettuce leaf or so or on chopped lettuce.

Note: Variations are interesting and infinite. Add capers, onion, pimiento, pickles, relish and even chili sauce to the mayonnaise or create your own surprise seasoning.

CREAMED CHICKEN AND HAM

1 tablespoon butter	⅓ cup diced ham (preferably country cured ham)
1 tablespoon flour	
1 can (about 13¾ ounces) chicken broth or freshly made broth to cover	½ cup diced, cooked chicken breast
	1 tablespoon heavy cream

1. Melt the butter in a small casserole, stir in the flour and add ½ cup broth. The broth may be reduced and enrich by boiling rapidly. Retain any extra broth for future use. Stir to eliminate lumps.
2. Add the diced ham and simmer 5 minutes.
3. Add the diced chicken, mix well, cover and keep warm until serving time. Stir in the cream just before serving.

Note: Serve over rice or cornbread.

CHICKEN A LA KING

1 tablespoon butter	¼ cup pimientos, diced
¼ cup mushrooms	1 egg yolk
1 tablespoon flour	1 tablespoon sherry
½ cup chicken broth	Salt and pepper
½ to ⅔ cup cooked chicken	

1. Melt the butter in a small casserole and sauté the mushrooms for 1 minute. Remove the mushrooms. Now stir the flour into the butter in the casserole and gradually add the chicken broth. Continue stirring until the sauce is smooth.
2. Add the chicken, pimientos, and mushrooms to the sauce and keep it warm.
3. At serving time, heat the casserole thoroughly and stir in the egg yolk, sherry, and season as necessary. Serve immediately.

Fish and Seafood

Boiled Shrimp • Shrimp Creole • Shrimp Curry
Scalloped Oysters • Broiled Salmon Steak
Simple Salmon Salad • Salmon and Rice Casserole
Salmon Cakes • Tuna Loaf
Skillet Clam Hash • Scalloped Clams

Fish is delightful and it's good for you, but I didn't find that out in the Midwest. It wasn't until I got to East Hampton that I really learned to like fish; out of the water in the morning and onto the table that noon or evening. Of course, we had Missouri River catfish at home, but I didn't take to it. And the bass didn't take to my hook at the Lake of the Ozarks nor did the trout in upstate New York.

Thus my fish cooking has been limited, but I have enjoyed preparing shrimp, oysters, salmon, and tuna. These shellfish, the canned tuna, and canned or fresh salmon have appeared many times in my kitchen.

BOILED SHRIMP

½ pound raw shrimp
1 lettuce leaf in bits or ¼ cup celery with leaves, diced

1 lemon slice
¼ teaspoon salt
3 peppercorns

1. Wash and drain shrimp in a colander
2. Place in a suitable-sized saucepan, add other ingredients and water to cover, and bring to a boil.
3. Add the shrimp to the boiling water and simmer for 3 minutes for small to medium shrimp; 4 or 5 minutes for large shrimp.
4. Let the shrimp cool in the cooking liquid.
5. Using small scissors or a sharp knife cut along the back rim of the shell and peel it off and discard.
6. Cut along the back of the peeled shrimp with a sharp knife and remove the dark vein or intestinal tract. Rinse under running cold water.
7. Refrigerate the cooked and cleaned shrimp until serving time.

Note: Serve with lemon juice, cocktail sauce, or ketchup and horseradish sauce or as shrimp creole (see recipe, below).

SHRIMP CREOLE

1 teaspoon oil
1 garlic clove, minced
2 ounces chopped onion
1½ ounces chopped green pepper
5 ounces chopped fresh tomatoes
¼ teaspoon parsley
Salt and freshly ground black pepper
½ bay leaf

¼ teaspoon thyme
¼ teaspoon worcestershire sauce
3 shakes Tabasco
1 teaspoon capers
¼ teaspoon sugar
3 ounces cooked, deveined shrimp (see recipe, above)
1 tablespoon butter

1. Heat the oil in a small casserole and sauté the garlic for 1 minute. Add the onion and cook stirring another minute or so until the onion becomes translucent.
2. Stir in the green pepper and cook another minute or so.
3. Add the chopped tomatoes and seasonings. Mix well and simmer until the green pepper is tender but not mushy.
4. Sauté the shrimp in butter on both sides for two minutes and add to the creole sauce. Serve hot over rice.

SHRIMP CURRY

⅓ pound shrimp or about 5 jumbo shrimp
1 tablespoon butter

½ cup curry sauce (see recipe, page 229)

1. Slit the back of the shrimp with a sharp knife or scissors and peel off the shell. Hold under cold water and let the pressure devein the shrimp. Help with the knife if necessary.
2. Melt the butter in a small skillet and add the shrimp. Cook over moderate heat stirring and turning for 2 or 3 minutes. Do not overcook.
3. Warm the sauce in a small casserole or covered pan and add the shrimp. Keep warm until serving time.

Note: Serve with rice and chutney.

SCALLOPED OYSTERS

1 tablespoon butter plus a little more to top the casserole
⅔ cup cracker crumbs
6 oysters (¾ cup) with liquid

¼ teaspoon salt
⅛ teaspoon paprika
1 tablespoon heavy cream

1. Melt the butter in a small casserole. Tilt and turn the casserole to coat the bottom and sides. Reserve any melted butter not required for this purpose to use in step 2.
2. Place half the crumbs on the bottom of the casserole and cover them with the oysters, salt, paprika, oyster liquid, cream and melted butter.
3. Finish the casserole with dry crumbs and dot with a little more butter.
4. Bake in the oven at 400 degrees for 20 minutes.

BROILED SALMON STEAK

½ pound salmon steak
Salt and freshly ground black pepper

2 tablespoons butter
¼ teaspoon chopped parsley
1 slice lemon

1. Season the salmon on both sides and let stand a few minutes.
2. Place the salmon on a sheet of aluminium foil on a suitable broiling pan or pie plate.
3. Cook the salmon for 3 minutes on each side under the broiler, buttering each side before broiling; use half the butter on each side.
4. Serve on a warm plate garnished with the lemon and parsley.

Note: This is excellent served with hollandaise sauce. See recipe, page 230.

SIMPLE SALMON SALAD

½ cup pink salmon (canned)
2 tablespoons India relish

2 tablespoons mayonnaise

1. Flake salmon in a small bowl removing dark skin and any small bones.
2. Add other ingredients and mix well. Serve on a bed of lettuce.

Note: Variations are unlimited: other types of relish may be substituted, sliced sweet pickles may be substituted or added, hard cooked eggs are good in this salad, lemon juice or herbs and seasonings may also be added.

SALMON AND RICE CASSEROLE

1 teaspoon melted butter
½ cup canned pink salmon with liquid
½ cup cooked rice
¼ teaspoon parsley flakes or minced fresh parsley

¼ teaspoon lemon juice
1 egg beaten
Salt
Dash of red pepper
Breadcrumbs

1. Butter bottom and sides of a small casserole
2. Mix all ingredients except breadcrumbs and add to the casserole
3. Top casserole with buttered bread crumbs
4. Bake in a 300 degree oven for 1 hour.
   Serve with lemon juice or lemon juice and melted butter, garnished with parsley.

SALMON CAKES

1 3¾-ounce can salmon
1 egg yolk
⅔ cup cracker crumbs
2 tablespoons heavy cream

1 teaspoon chopped parsley
Salt and pepper
1 tablespoon butter

1. Mix well all ingredients except the butter. Let the mixture stand ½ hour or so.
2. Form a cake of the mixture.
3. Heat the butter in a skillet and sauté the cake at low heat for 15 minutes. Turn and cook the other side 5 minutes. Serve hot with lemon wedges.

TUNA LOAF

1 3¼-ounce can white tuna
½ cup cracker crumbs
1 egg yolk
Salt and pepper

2 tablespoons heavy cream
1 teaspoon chopped parsley
1 tablespoon chopped onion
1 teaspoon butter

1. Mix all ingredients except the butter and mold into a small loaf.
2. Melt the butter in a small casserole with cover.
3. When ready to cook, place the loaf in the casserole and cover. Cook over a flame tamer at low heat or in an oven at 300 degrees for 1 hour. Turn the loaf during the last 15 minutes or when a nice crust has formed on the top.

SKILLET CLAM HASH

1 teaspoon butter
1 small onion, chopped
1 cup loosely packed cooked potatoes, finely diced
1 7½-ounce can minced clams

2 tablespoons cream (or milk if you are counting calories)
Salt and freshly ground black pepper

1. Melt the butter in a small skillet and sauté the onion until golden brown, not burned.
2. Add the diced potatoes, stir and cook a few minutes lifting the ingredients frequently to prevent sticking.
3. Drain the clams well and discard the clam juice. Then spread the drained clams evenly over the sautéed onion and potatoes.
4. Add the cream and season with salt and pepper.
5. Cook over low heat until the ingredients bubble. Serve immediately.

SCALLOPED CLAMS

4 teaspoons butter
1 6½-ounce can clams
⅔ cup cracker crumbs

Salt
½ teaspoon paprika
¼ cup cream

1. With 1 teaspoon of the butter coat well an ovenproof cooking dish.
2. Layer crumbs, and drained clams ending with a layer of crumbs in the cooking dish. Season each layer as you go.
3. Pour over the casserole ¼ cup of the clam juice and then the cream (light cream will be good, but heavy cream is much richer).
4. Dot the remaining butter on top of the casserole and place it in an oven preheated to 400 degrees. Cook 20 minutes.

Pasta and Rice

Linguini with Clam Sauce • Linguini Cheese and Cream
Spaghetti alla Carbonara • Chili Spaghetti
Salmon-Mushroom-Spaghetti Casserole
Chicken, Mushroom, and Cheese Spaghetti
Spaghetti with Ham and Mushrooms
Spaghetti with Anchovy Sauce
Macaroni and Cheese • Macaroni Casserole
Macaroni Casserole with Ham and Green Pepper
Creamed Ham, Macaroni, and Cheese
Pastitsio (Pasta with Meat, Greek Style)
Rice in Chicken Broth • Rice Creole • Lonesome Rice
Risotto Milanese (Rice with Saffron, Wine, and Cheese)
Rice with Saffron

In my childhood encounter with pasta I acquired the erroneous idea that pasta with cheese was macaroni and that pasta with a tomato-meat sauce was spaghetti. That was long ago and I have since discovered that pasta shapes determine the name of the dish.

Pasta has a large following and I have been in line a long time. Even in Algiers during World War II, I made it for friends who were very accommodating and ingenious in helping to locate the needed ingredients. I remember one crisis. There were no onions in the market. It was only after a tour of the streets in the jeep that I spied a vendor with a large bunch of leeks. I haven't made spaghetti with leeks instead of onions before or since. It was an unusual recipe, but we ate it all.

In Rome pasta is usually a few ounces of goodness before the main dish. For me it is frequently a quarter pound portion and quite enough for the principal part of a meal. In American restaurants one can usually count on a great pile of pasta, much too much for one serving unless you have dug a ditch, or plan to have no other dish at this meal, or you don't mind being uncomfortable afterwards.

I suggest dividing a one-pound package of spaghetti, spaghettini, or linguini into 4 parts ¼ pound each. Tie each section with a piece of string or wire tie so that you can easily determine a suitable portion. A quarter pound of spaghetti is just over 100 strands and not too much for a main course.

The Algerian recipe with leeks I have not retained, but the pasta recipes which are included in this book are highly recommended. I also include several dishes using another grain, rice.

LINGUINI WITH CLAM SAUCE

1 tablespoon oil	3 quarts of water
1 garlic clove, finely minced	1 teaspoon salt
2 tablespoons chopped parsley	¼ pound linguini
4 ounces minced clams and juice (or a 6½-ounce can)	

1. Heat the oil in a skillet and sauté the garlic for 1 minute stirring to prevent browning. Add the parsley and continue cooking another minute or so stirring all the while.
2. Add the minced clams and juice and continue the cooking for 5 minutes stirring occasionally.
3. Bring the water to a galloping boil and add the salt and linguini. Cook about 5 minutes, drain and rinse.
4. Transfer the clam mixture to the kettle in which the linguini was cooked; add the drained linguini and mix well over low heat. Cover and cook until the linguini is done to your taste, about 5 minutes to al dente. Serve hot.

LINGUINI CHEESE AND CREAM

¼ pound linguini	Salt and freshly ground black pepper
¾ cup grated Parmesan cheese	
¼ pint heavy cream	

1. Cook linguini in boiling water about 10 minutes or according to directions on the package.
2. Drain linguini and add some butter or oil to prevent sticking.
3. Toss pasta in a warm pan or chafing dish adding cheese, cream, and seasonings a little at a time to the desired consistency.

SPAGHETTI ALLA CARBONARA

4 slices bacon cut in ½-inch strips or ¼ pound prosciutto or ham in fine dice
1 small onion, finely chopped
¼ pound spaghetti

1 tablespoon butter
1 egg yolk
2 tablespoons cream
¼ cup Parmesan cheese, grated
Salt and pepper

1. Cook the bacon in a small skillet until crisp. Drain on paper towels and reserve.
2. Pour most of the bacon fat out of the skillet and sauté the onion until wilted.
3. Cook the spaghetti until tender in at least 2 quarts of rapidly boiling salted water (about 10 minutes). Separate the strands with a two pronged fork to prevent sticking together.
4. Drain the spaghetti in a colander and rinse with a little water. Add the butter to the cooking vessel and coat all sides before returning the spaghetti to the pot.
5. Mix the egg yolk and the cream and pour over the spaghetti in the pot. Add the bacon, cheese, and wilted onion.
6. Toss well and serve hot.

CHILI SPAGHETTI

⅛ pound spaghetti (about 50 strands)
1 teaspoon butter

1 cup chili (see recipe, page 59)
¼ cup Parmesan cheese, grated

1. Drop the spaghetti into 2 quarts of boiling water and cook 10 minutes. Drain and rinse with cold water.
2. Add butter to the kettle in which the spaghetti was cooked. When the butter melts, coat the bottom and sides of the kettle. Return the spaghetti to the buttered kettle.
3. Add the chili to the spaghetti and mix well.
4. When ready to serve, reheat the spaghetti and serve hot with grated cheese.

SALMON-MUSHROOM-SPAGHETTI CASSEROLE

2 tablespoons butter	Salt and freshly ground black
¼ cup sliced mushrooms	pepper
1 tablespoon flour	Two shakes each nutmeg and
½ cup half-and-half	red pepper
1 3¾-ounce can salmon	¼ pound spaghetti
	¼ cup grated Parmesan cheese

1. Sauté mushrooms in half the butter for 1 minute and reserve.
2. Melt remaining butter in a saucepan, stir in the flour, cook for 1 minute and add the half-and-half stirring rapidly with a wire whisk.
3. Drain the salmon and reserve the liquid. Discard skin and bones and flake the salmon.
4. When the sauce thickens, add salmon liquid, mushrooms, and finally the salmon and seasonings. Mix well and keep warm.
5. Cook the spaghetti 10 minutes in rapidly boiling water to which you have added a bit of salt. Drain well and rinse in cold water.
6. Place half the spaghetti in a small buttered casserole, add the salmon mixture and cover with the remaining spaghetti. Top with Parmesan cheese and bake uncovered in a 350-degree oven for 20 minutes.

CHICKEN, MUSHROOM, AND CHEESE SPAGHETTI

½ chicken breast	4 ounces spaghetti
¾ cup chicken broth	6 mushrooms, sliced
1 small onion, diced	1 tablespoon butter
2 tablespoons finely chopped celery	1 tablespoon flour
Salt and pepper	½ cup grated cheddar cheese
2 quarts of water	1 tablespoon tomato puree (optional)

1. Place chicken, broth, onion, celery, salt and pepper in a small pan. Bring to a boil and simmer 20 minutes. Allow the chicken to cool in the liquid. Remove bones, skin and dice the chicken.
2. Bring the water and about 1 teaspoon of salt to a boil in a kettle and add the spaghetti. When the water returns to a boil, cook 5 minutes and drain.
3. Mix the cooked spaghetti and diced chicken with the mushrooms in a lightly buttered saucepan or small casserole.
4. Melt the remaining butter in another pan and stir in the flour. Mix well and add the cooking liquid first and then the cheese while stirring rapidly with a wire whisk to incorporate the butter-flour mixture and produce a thickened sauce. Stir in the tomato puree if desired.
5. Pour the sauce over the spaghetti-chicken casserole and bake uncovered in a 350 degree oven for 20 minutes.

SPAGHETTI WITH HAM AND MUSHROOMS

3 ounces spaghetti	1 garlic clove, minced
2 quarts water	1 ounce ham or prosciutto, minced
A pinch of salt	minced
1 teaspoon butter	6 small mushrooms, sliced
1 tablespoon oil	½ cup tomato sauce
1 tablespoon minced onion	2 tablespoons grated Parmesan cheese
1 tablespoon minced shallots	cheese

1. Boil the water and add the spaghetti and salt. Cook for 10 minutes. Drain in a colander and rinse with cold water. Butter the cooking pan and return the spaghetti and keep warm.
2. In the oil, sauté the onion, shallots, and garlic for about 2 minutes.
3. Add the ham and continue the cooking another 2 minutes. Stir well during the cooking.

4. Now add the mushrooms and tomato sauce and simmer another minute. Place over a flame tamer and keep warm until serving time.
5. Place the spaghetti on a warm platter and pour over the sauce and cheese. Add more cheese if desired.

SPAGHETTI WITH ANCHOVY SAUCE

1 tablespoon olive oil	1 teaspoon chopped basil
1 garlic clove, minced	1 anchovy fillet
1 cup peeled, seeded, chopped tomatoes	¼ pound spaghetti

1. Heat the oil in a skillet and cook the garlic for 1 minute
2. Add the tomatoes and basil and simmer 15 minutes.
3. Empty the anchovy into a saucepan and cook stirring until melted. Combine with the tomato sauce and keep warm.
4. Cook the spaghetti in boiling water for 15 minutes or to the desired doneness. Drain in a colander and rinse in cool water.
5. Add the sauce to the spaghetti, mix well and serve in a warm plate.

MACARONI AND CHEESE

⅓ cup elbow macaroni	½ cup milk
2 quarts water	1 cup grated cheddar cheese
1 teaspoon salt	6 drops worcestershire sauce
1½ tablespoons butter	Paprika (optional)
1 tablespoon flour	

1. Cook macaroni in rapidly boiling salted water for 6 minutes and drain well in a colander.
2. Melt 1 tablespoon of the butter in a saucepan, stir in the flour

and add the milk all at once. Stir well with a wire whisk until the sauce is smooth and beginning to thicken. Add the cheese and worcestershire sauce and blend well.

3. Use the remaining butter to coat a small casserole. Add the macaroni and the cheese sauce, stir well and shake a few grains of paprika on the surface.

4. Bake uncovered in a 350 degree oven for ½ hour. Serve hot.

MACARONI CASSEROLE

⅔	cup macaroni	3	ounces ground round steak
1	quart water	3	teaspoons butter
1	teaspoon oil	1	tablespoon flour
½	cup chopped onion	½	cup milk
½	garlic clove, minced	1	tablespoon grated cheese,
1	tablespoon tomato paste		cheddar or Parmesan
	Salt and pepper		

1. Cook the macaroni for 9 minutes in rapidly boiling salted water. Do not overcook.

2. Drain in a colander, rinse, and reserve.

3. Heat the oil in a skillet and cook the onion and garlic for a few minutes stirring constantly. Add tomato paste, and season with salt and pepper.

4. Add the ground round and continue stirring until it loses its reddish color. Remove from the fire.

5. Use 1 teaspoon of the butter to grease a small casserole. Arrange in the buttered casserole a layer of half the macaroni, then a layer of the seasoned ground round, and finish with the remainder of the macaroni.

6. In a small pan melt the remaining butter and stir in the flour. Add the milk all at once and stir continuously with a wire whisk until the sauce begins to thicken.

7. Pour the sauce over the casserole and top with the cheese. Bake at 350 degrees for 20 minutes.

MACARONI CASSEROLE WITH HAM AND GREEN PEPPER

⅓ cup macaroni
¼ cup ham in ¼-inch dice
(preferably country smoked ham or prosciutto)
¼ cup diced green pepper

1 tablespoon butter
1 tablespoon flour
½ cup light cream or milk
¼ cup grated Parmesan cheese

1. In about a quart of boiling salted water cook the macaroni for 9 minutes.
2. Drain and rinse the cooked macaroni in cold water and reserve.
3. Sauté the ham and green pepper, stirring frequently, for 3 minutes.
4. In another saucepan melt the butter and stir in the flour. Cook for a minute or so and add the milk all at once stirring vigorously with a wire whisk. Continue until the sauce begins to thicken.
5. Grease a small casserole with ham fat, oil or butter and add the macaroni.
6. Stir the sauce into the pan where the ham and green pepper have cooked and scrape into the sauce the brown particles that have formed on the bottom and side of the pan.
7. Pour the well mixed sauce over the macaroni, top with the cheese. When ready to serve, place under a hot broiler for several minutes or until the top of the casserole is light brown. Serve very hot.

CREAMED HAM, MACARONI, AND CHEESE

½ cup macaroni
1 teaspoon butter
1 teaspoon flour
¼ cup cream

Pepper
⅓ cup diced cheddar cheese
⅓ cup diced ham (preferably country cured ham)

1. Cook the macaroni in boiling water for 7 minutes. Drain in a colander and rinse in cold water.
2. Melt the butter in a small casserole and stir in the flour and lastly the cream. Stir until well blended and no lumps of flour remain.
3. Stir in the cheese and continue stirring until the cheese is melted. Add a little milk or water if the sauce becomes too thick. Cover and keep warm.
4. Sauté the ham for about 3 minutes depending on the size of the dice. The ham should be cooked but not browned.
5. Combine macaroni, ham and sauce and mix well in the casserole or covered saucepan. Cover and place over a flame tamer with low heat until serving time.

PASTITSIO
(Pasta with Meat, Greek Style)

3 ounces macaroni or your favorite noodles	1 pinch each of cinnamon, oregano, and nutmeg
2 tablespoons chopped onion	Salt and pepper
2 tablespoons butter plus enough to butter the baking dish	1 tablespoon flour
	½ cup milk
4 ounces ground chuck or round steak	¼ cup cream
	1 egg yolk, beaten
⅓ cup tomato puree	¼ cup freshly grated Parmesan cheese

1. Cook the pasta in rapidly boiling salted water for 5 minutes. Drain and rinse in a colander.
2. Heat half the butter in a skillet and sauté the onion until wilted. Add the meat and stir to break it up into small pieces. Cook the meat until the red color is replaced with grey. Add the tomato puree and spices and continue cooking for about 5 minutes.
3. Melt the rest of the butter in a small casserole and stir in the flour. Cook 1 minute. Add the milk all at once and stir with a

wire whisk until it begins to thicken.

4. Combine the cream and egg yolk and mix well. Add this to the flour and milk mixture and bring just to a boil.
5. In a buttered ovenproof dish, layer first the meat mixture and then pasta. Repeat once. Pour the sauce over the layers, sprinkle with Parmesan, cover and bake 45 minutes in a 375 degree oven. Uncover the vessel for the last 15 minutes of cooking.

RICE IN CHICKEN BROTH

¾ cup chicken broth
1 small onion, diced

Salt and pepper
¼ cup uncooked rice

1. Bring the chicken broth, onion, salt and pepper to a boil.
2. Add the rice, cover and reduce the heat to the lowest.
3. Stir occasionally and cook until the broth is absorbed.

RICE CREOLE

¼ cup rice
⅔ cup tomato juice
2 tablespoons chopped onion

2 tablespoons chopped green pepper
Salt and pepper

1. Place all ingredients in a small casserole with cover.
2. Stir well and bring to a boil.
3. Bake in the oven at 350 degrees for 20 minutes.

LONESOME RICE

½ cup water
¼ teaspoon salt

¼ cup rice (Uncle Ben's converted is best)

1. Bring the water to a boil in a saucepan or small casserole with a tight fitting lid, add the salt.
2. Stir in the rice, return to a boil and cover tightly.
3. Reduce heat to lowest and cook 20 minutes or until the water is absorbed and the rice is done.

Note: This rice may be prepared a little in advance and warmed just before serving.

RISOTTO MILANESE
(Rice with Saffron, Wine, and Cheese)

1 cup chicken broth
1 pinch leaf saffron, chopped
1 tablespoon chopped onion
1 tablespoon butter
   Salt
⅓ cup rice

¼ cup dry white wine or vermouth
¼ cup freshly grated Parmesan cheese
   Freshly ground pepper

1. Heat the chicken broth just to the boil and turn off the flame.
2. In a small muffin cup or other container place the saffron and cover it with a small portion of hot broth. Set aside.
3. In a small casserole or covered pan sauté the onion in butter until wilted, add salt and rice and stir to prevent browning. Add saffron mixture and wine.
4. Add the remainder of hot broth, stir, cover and cook over lowest heat until the rice is tender and the liquid is absorbed.
5. Stir in the cheese and sprinkle with pepper. Serve hot.

RICE WITH SAFFRON

1 tablespoon butter	½ bay leaf
1 garlic clove, minced	⅓ cup rice
2 tablespoons onion, chopped	Salt
¼ teaspoon saffron	⅔ cup chicken broth

1. Melt the butter in a small casserole or other pan with a tight fitting cover and sauté the garlic over low heat a second or so and add the onion. Stir and cook until the onion becomes translucent, a minute or so.
2. Add the saffron, bay leaf and rice. Mix well and cook stirring for 1 minute.
3. Salt to taste and pour in the chicken broth. Continue stirring and bring to a boil.
4. Cover tightly and place in the oven for 20 minutes, at 400 degrees.

Mostly Eggs and Omelets

Spanish Omelet • Spinach Omelet • Garden Breakfast
Egg à la Russe • Fried Egg Beurre Noir
Eggs with Ham-Tomato Sauce
Deviled Egg • French Toast
Cheese Soufflé • Corn Soufflé

Books have been written about the egg and about omelets. I haven't done that. My lack of attention to this great food is not at all a lack of appreciation. I enjoy eggs. I could have them each morning with relish and how nice is a stuffed, deviled egg on a picnic.

The typical morning egg dishes have been skipped here. I believe their successful preparation comes with practice. I do include here a few omelet and soufflé recipes. These can be varied infinitely by the substitution of another ingredient for the particular dish mentioned.

The several other egg dishes included here are particular favorites.

SPANISH OMELET

1 medium tomato	½ cup green pepper, diced
1½ tablespoons butter	Salt and pepper
¼ cup onion, diced	2 eggs

1. Dip the tomato in boiling water for 10 seconds to loosen the skin, then peel it. Core and cut it in half and press holding the cut side down to release the seeds. Chop the tomato in small dice.
2. Melt ½ tablespoon of the butter in a pan and sauté the onion until wilted. Add the green pepper and finally the tomato and seasonings. Simmer stirring occasionally about 10 minutes. This is the filling for the omelet.
3. Break the eggs into a bowl and beat until the yolks are well blended with the whites. Add salt and pepper.
4. Heat the remaining butter in a skillet or an omelet pan until the butter bubbles and is just about to brown.
5. Immediately add the eggs after one final beat and stir rapidly to bring the entire mixture to the same temperature. Tip the side of the pan to allow any excess liquid egg to reach the warmer portion of the pan. Keep tilting until all the egg is set.
6. Place the filling on one side of the omelet, and slide the omelet onto a hot plate flipping the unfilled side of the omelet over the filling.
7. Slide a pat of butter over the surface of the omelet and serve hot.

Note: Be advised that the quantities need not be exact. One small onion and one small tomato will do very well. Also your own taste may guide you in a heavier hand with green pepper, or hot pepper or whatever you like to emphasize.

SPINACH OMELET

2 tablespoons butter	1 tablespoon chicken broth
1 tablespoon chopped onion	2 eggs
2 tablespoons cooked spinach	Salt and pepper

1. In half the butter cook the onion until translucent and add the spinach. Continue cooking and add the broth. Stir and cook for 1 or 2 minutes. Keep warm.
2. Break eggs into a bowl, add salt to taste and stir to mix well.
3. Melt the remaining butter in an omelet pan or small skillet over high heat to almost smoking.
4. After an extra beat add the eggs to the skillet and stir rapidly once or twice tilting the skillet to allow liquid egg to reach the hot surface of the pan. Shake the skillet to prevent the eggs from sticking.
5. Quickly add the onion-spinach mixture to one side of the cooking eggs.
6. Slide the eggs immediately from the tilted skillet into a warm plate flipping the unfilled side of the omelet over the spinach filling.
7. Serve with a pat of butter on top and a sprinkle of freshly ground pepper.

GARDEN BREAKFAST
(Vegetables and Egg)

½ teaspoon oil	½ tablespoon green pepper, diced
½ cup cubed rutabaga or turnip	
1 small onion, sliced	1 egg
1 carrot, sliced	Salt and pepper

1. Pour the oil into a small casserole with cover and add the vegetables in layers one at a time. Salt and pepper the casserole.

2. Cover the casserole and simmer until the vegetables are tender (about 20 minutes).
3. Uncover the casserole and break the egg on top. When the egg is set, serve immediately.

Note: Various vegetable combinations, almost anything you have fresh, may be used to good advantage in this delightful breakfast or light lunch.

EGG A LA RUSSE

1 egg	1 pinch each salt, pepper, and
½ cup shredded lettuce	sugar
1 tablespoon mayonnaise	¼ teaspoon lemon juice
1 tablespoon tomato ketchup	1 teaspoon capers

1. Place the egg is a small pan and cover with cold water. Place over heat and bring to a boil; reduce heat and simmer 15 minutes. Plunge the cooked egg immediately into cold water to make peeling easy.
2. Arrange the shredded lettuce on a serving plate and top with the egg which has been peeled and sliced in half. Refrigerate.
3. Mix well the remaining ingredients or shake them together in a small jar.
4. At serving time, mask the egg halves with the sauce and enjoy as a first course or as a salad.

Note: It's even more deserving of its name with a little caviar mixed in the sauce or with a small amount topping each egg half.

FRIED EGG BEURRE NOIR

1 egg	1 teaspoon chopped parsley
1 tablespoon butter	¼ teaspoon vinegar

1. Fry the egg in half the butter and place on a warm plate.
2. Add the remaining butter to the frying pan and the chopped parsley. Cook very slowly until the butter is a rich brown. Pour over the egg.
3. Add the vinegar to the frying pan and cook a minute or so. Pour over the egg and serve.

EGGS WITH HAM-TOMATO SAUCE

¼ cup diced ham
1 teaspoon butter or oil or rendered ham fat
1 tablespoon chopped parsley

½ cup canned tomatoes, drained and diced
¼ teaspoon sugar (vary according to the acidity of tomatoes)

1. Sauté ham in fat for 1 minute.
2. Add parsley and cook another minute, then add tomatoes and sugar.
3. Cook until liquid is almost evaporated.
4. Serve with scrambled eggs or in an omelet.

DEVILED EGG

1 egg
½ teaspoon wine vinegar
1 pinch dry mustard
¼ teaspoon lemon juice
1 pinch salt

1 shake red pepper
¼ teaspoon minced parsley
⅛ teaspoon sugar
2 capers

1. Place the egg gently in boiling water. When the water returns to a boil, cook the egg for 10 minutes. Immediately plunge the egg into cold water. Crack the shell well against the side of the sink and remove it under cold water.

2. Cut the peeled egg in half and carefully scoop out the yolk into a small bowl.
3. Add to the bowl all seasonings (except capers) and mix well.
4. Stuff the egg halves with the seasoned yolk and place a caper on top of each.

Note: Vary the seasonings according to your taste. For a variation, add mayonnaise, onion, shallots, pimiento, etc.

FRENCH TOAST

1 egg	Parsley flakes
Salt and pepper	1 tablespoon butter
1 slice white bread	

1. Break the egg in a saucer, add the salt and pepper and beat until combined.
2. Place the bread in the egg mixture and allow to soak up the egg first on one side, then on the other. Sprinkle with parsley.
3. Melt the butter in a small pan and add the egg-soaked bread.
4. Cook slowly for 1 minute on one side and then turn. Remove to a warm plate after a half minute on the second side. Do not overcook. Serve immediately.

CHEESE SOUFFLE

1 tablespoon butter	1 drop Tabasco
1 tablespoon flour	1 egg
½ cup milk	3 tablespoons grated cheddar
Salt and freshly ground black pepper	cheese

1. Heat the butter in a small pan and add the flour, stir and mix well. Cook 1 minute.

2. Add the milk all at once stirring vigorously with a wire whisk. Add the salt, pepper, and Tabasco, continue mixing.
3. Cook until the mixture begins to thicken and is rid of lumps.
4. Break the egg and drop the white into a small cup or oven-proof bowl. Place the yolk in another small container.
5. Add a tablespoon or so of the white sauce to the yolk and mix well. Pour this into the remaining white sauce and stir well.
6. Beat the egg white with a rotary beater until it forms stiff peaks.
7. Pour the thickened white sauce into a greased casserole or other suitable ovenproof vessel*; stir in the grated cheese and mix well.
8. Carefully fold in the stiff egg white and bake at 400 degrees for 20 minutes or until the top of the uncovered dish is brown.

* Use a small soufflé pan or at least a straight-sided small casserole so that the soufflé can rise unimpeded up the straight sides of the container while cooking.

CORN SOUFFLE

1 ear cooked corn	1 tablespoon flour
1 teaspoon minced onion	1 egg
¾ cup milk	Salt and pepper
1 tablespoon butter plus a little to butter the baking dish	

1. Cut the corn kernels from the cob and mix them well with the onion and ¼ cup of the milk.
2. Melt the butter and stir in the flour. Cook 1 minute or so and add the remaining milk. Stir constantly with a wire whisk until well blended and beginning to thicken.
3. Add the corn and onion blend. Stir again.
4. Separate the egg and incorporate the yolk into the sauce. Add salt and pepper.
5. Beat the egg white to stiff and fold it into sauce. Put into a buttered soufflé dish or small casserole.
6. Bake the soufflé uncovered in the oven for 20 minutes at 400 degrees.

Vegetables

Asparagus Vinaigrette • Home-Style Green Beans
Green Beans Jessie Lee • Mixed Bean Salad
Kidney Bean Salad • Harvard Beets
Broccoli with Cheese Sauce • Cabbage Slaw • Cole Slaw
Red Cabbage • Thanksgiving Carrots
French-Style Carrots • Braised Cauliflower
Braised Celery • Celery and Stewed Tomatoes
Puree of Celery Root and Potatoes • Corn on the Cob
Fresh Corn and Green Pepper • Corn and Tomatoes
Corn and Celery • Corn Casserole
Corn Casserole and Tortilla Chips • Corn and Tomatoes Sauté
Eggplant Casserole • Eggplant, Quick and Good
Eggplant Stew • Moussaka
Eggplant and Cheese Casserole
Eggplant with Rice and Cumin • Braised Endive
Braised Endive and Bacon • White Onion Special
French Peas • Green Pepper Stuffed with Fresh Corn
Pomme de Terre Budapest • Hot Potato Salad with Bacon
Fried Potatoes Thinly Sliced
Potato, Egg, and Cheese Casserole • Scalloped Potatoes
Scalloped Potatoes with Garlic and Cheese
Ratatouille • Spinach
Tomato Stuffed with Corn • Zucchini, Potatoes, and Tomatoes
Zucchini and Vegetable Casserole
Zucchini Cheese Casserole • Zucchini with Tomatoes
Zucchini Provençale • Smothered Fresh Vegetables
Sherry Kraut

I like vegetables. I almost always have. Of course as a child I remember I wasn't particularly fond of carrots, spinach, or tomatoes, especially when they were so plentiful in the garden just behind the house, but I got over that. Now those vegetables are actually among my favorites.

But my fondest memory of vegetables dates back to the day I returned from the World War II to my home in Missouri. On this occasion my cousin prepared a dinner for three of us, just family, a vegetable dinner. A vegetable dinner, because in those days there was a shortage of meat. Vegetable dinners became very popular; they can be very good and patriotic too. But anyway, after army food for four years, which wasn't bad but I mean it was *not* home cooking, that vegetable dinner was unforgettably delicious. The circumstances, the freshness of the local produce, the careful cooking all registered approval in my mind; approval and praise remain in my memory. My mouth still waters when I think of the green beans cooked with a little country ham, boiled onions with fresh country butter, fresh beets with butter and pepper, and, oh yes, there was a hard-boiled egg which was good as contrast.

So I have recorded many of the vegetable recipes that I have prepared over the years and I recommend them highly. Just one caution. I feel very strongly that one should gauge very carefully the amount of salt added to vegetables; one's own tolerance is important. Just the right amount to satisfy one's own taste and on the low side. I think it is too bad to hide or overpower the taste of vegetables with too much salt. A little, yes, but be sure to taste before adding salt. Too much salt in a normal climate is not good for the health either.

ASPARAGUS VINAIGRETTE

5 medium asparagus spears	½ teaspoon Dijon mustard
Salt	Freshly ground black pepper
2 tablespoons olive oil or vegetable oil	½ teaspoon shallots, finely minced
½ teaspoon wine vinegar	¼ teaspoon minced parsley

1. Trim the asparagus to within 1 inch or so of the tips with a potato peeler. Cut off and discard the tough lower sections.
2. Place the asparagus in a suitable pan, cover with water, salt to taste and simmer until tender to the touch of a fork.
3. Assemble all other ingredients in a small jar with tight fitting top and shake to mix well.
4. Drain the cooked asparagus and place on the serving plate. Shake the sauce again and pour over the asparagus.
5. Serve at room temperature.

HOME STYLE GREEN BEANS

¼ pound green beans	2 tablespoons bacon or country ham fat or scraps of ham, bacon or a ham hock
1 medium onion, halved	Freshly ground black pepper

1. Break the ends off beans, draw any strings and break into 1-inch lengths.
2. Wash well, drain, and cover with water.
3. Add the other ingredients and simmer 2 to 3 hours covered. Add additional water if necessary.

GREEN BEANS JESSIE LEE

2 slices bacon, diced	1 tablespoon sugar
¼ cup diced onion	1 cup loosely packed cooked
¼ cup vinegar	green beans

1. Cook the bacon slowly until it is crisp, adding the onion toward the end of the cooking.
2. Tip the skillet and remove all excess fat or strain the bacon and onion discarding the liquid fat.
3. To the skillet add the vinegar and sugar and stir to incorporate the particles sticking to the bottom of the pan. Boil 1 minute or so and pour over the beans in a casserole or covered pan.
4. Warm thoroughly and mix well just before serving.

Note: Serve warm as a vegetable dish; serve cold on lettuce for a salad.

MIXED BEAN SALAD

½ cup white vinegar	1 8-ounce can wax beans
½ cup water	1 8-ounce can kidney beans
½ cup sugar or a bit less	2 medium onions, chopped
¼ cup vegetable oil	freshly ground black pepper
1 8-ounce can green beans	

1. Boil vinegar, water, sugar and oil for 5 minutes.
2. Place drained beans and chopped onion in a bowl and pour over them the warm liquid.
3. Refrigerate and serve.

Note: Serve on lettuce as a salad or plain as a relish. This recipe makes three or four individual servings. The salad improves with time and may be kept for up to 2 weeks in the refrigerator.

KIDNEY BEAN SALAD

2 tablespoons canned kidney beans

2 tablespoons chopped onion

1 tablespoon chopped sweet gherkins or sweet pickle relish

1 tablespoon mayonnaise

Mix all ingredients well and refrigerate for 1 hour or so before serving on lettuce.

HARVARD BEETS

1 tablespoon sugar

1 teaspoon cornstarch

1 tablespoon vinegar

2 tablespoons beet cooking liquid or water

½ cup cooked or canned beets, cubed (see note)

1 teaspoon butter

1. Combine the sugar, cornstarch, vinegar and liquid. Stir until thickened and smooth over low heat.
2. Add the cubed beets and butter and heat thoroughly. Serve hot as a side dish.

Note: Cook beets in lightly salted water to cover until tender to a fork. Any leftover beets above the volume needed for this recipe may be put to good use in the near future as pickled beets, sliced in a salad with onion, or in a dozen other ways.

BROCCOLI WITH CHEESE SAUCE

1 stalk broccoli, washed, picked
    over and trimmed
    Salt
1 tablespoon butter

1 tablespoon flour
½ cup milk
½ cup grated cheddar cheese

1. Place the broccoli in a saucepan and cover with lightly salted water. Simmer to tender. Drain.
2. Melt the butter in a saucepan, stir in the flour and pour in the milk all at once stirring vigorously with a wire whisk until the sauce begins to thicken.
3. Stir in the cheese and test for seasoning. You may want more salt.
4. Cover the cheese sauce and when ready to serve, heat it for a minute or so and pour over the broccoli. You may wish to serve it in a separate plate or bowl to conserve the integrity of the sauce.

CABBAGE SLAW

1 tablespoon finely minced onion
1 tablespoon mayonnaise
½ teaspoon mustard
2 drops worcestershire sauce

2 tablespoons cream
¼ teaspoon celery seed
1 cup cabbage, shredded

1. Mix well all ingredients except the cabbage.
2. Place the shredded cabbage in a bowl; pour the other ingredients over the cabbage and blend well.
3. Refrigerate and serve cold.

COLE SLAW

½ cup finely chopped or shredded cabbage (it may be all or part red cabbage)

¼ teaspoon celery seed

1 tablespoon (more or less to your taste) french dressing, mayonnaise, or vinegar and sugar mixed to your taste

Salt

1. Soak the cabbage for 1 hour in ice water to cover.
2. Drain the cabbage in a sieve and place on paper towels to dry. Wrap the towels over the cabbage to aid in drying. Chill in the refrigerator.
3. At serving time sprinkle the celery seed over the cabbage, add the dressing or vinegar and mix thoroughly. Check for seasoning. You may want more salt. If so, mix it in well and serve.

RED CABBAGE

2 teaspoons butter

2 tablespoons chopped onion

2 tablespoons brown sugar

2 tablespoons cider vinegar

1 cup shredded red cabbage

1. Sauté the onion lightly in the butter.
2. Add the brown sugar and vinegar. Stir.
3. Add the cabbage, cover and simmer 40 minutes.
4. At serving time, reheat and serve warm.

THANKSGIVING CARROTS

2 carrots

1 small baking potato

1 small sweet potato

Salt and pepper

Nutmeg

1 tablespoon butter

1. Peel and dice the vegetables. Cover with water and simmer to tender.
2. Puree the vegetables by using a food mill, sieve, or ricer.
3. Season the puree with salt and pepper, nutmeg, and add the butter.
4. Mix well and keep hot to serving time.

FRENCH-STYLE CARROTS
(Vichy)

2 carrots (about ¼ pound peeled)	1 tablespoon butter
	Salt and pepper
¼ teaspoon sugar	2 tablespoons chopped onion
2 tablespoons water	Parsley to garnish

1. Cut the carrots into very thin slices. Place the carrots in a skillet and add remaining ingredients.
2. Cover the skillet with a sheet of wax paper and cook shaking from time to time over low heat until the carrots are fork tender (about 10 minutes).
3. Sprinkle with parsley and serve.

BRAISED CAULIFLOWER

1 tablespoon onion, chopped	¼ teaspoon cumin
1 teaspoon vegetable oil	⅛ teaspoon salt
5 ounces (according to appetite) cauliflower in flowerets	⅛ teaspoon freshly ground black pepper
¼ teaspoon turmeric	2 tablespoons water

1. Sauté the onion in the oil about 5 minutes stirring.
2. Add the cauliflower and other ingredients, bring to a boil and cover. Simmer about 20 minutes or until the cauliflower is tender. Stir several times to incorporate the seasonings. Add more water if needed to keep the cauliflower moist and un-burned.

BRAISED CELERY

1 heart of celery (see note)	A pinch of salt
½ teaspoon lemon juice	1 tablespoon water
2 tablespoons butter	¼ teaspoon sugar

1. Wash the celery and tie with a string to keep it together during the cooking.
2. Place the celery in a pan with a cover that fits tightly and add the lemon juice, half the butter, the salt, water and sugar.
3. Bring to a boil covered and cook over moderate heat about 30 minutes or until the celery is tender.
4. Drain the celery and brown in the remaining butter to a caramel color.

Note: Several ribs of celery may be tied together to resemble a heart.

CELERY AND STEWED TOMATOES

2 celery ribs, trimmed and diced	1 8-ounce can stewed tomatoes
	1 tablespoon minced onion

1. Place all ingredients in a small casserole or stewing pan and simmer ½ hour.
2. Taste and correct the seasoning by the addition of salt and pepper if desired.

PUREE OF CELERY ROOT AND POTATOES

3 ounces potatoes	1 teaspoon butter
3 ounces celery root	1 tablespoon heavy cream
Salt and pepper	

1. Cover the potatoes and celery root with water. Add the salt and pepper and cook until tender, about 15 minutes.
2. Puree the vegetables by passing through a food mill or potato ricer or push them through a sieve.
3. Add the butter and cream and mix thoroughly; test for seasoning and add more salt if you desire. Keep warm and heat over a flame tamer just before serving.

CORN ON THE COB

3 quarts water	1 or 2 ears corn
1 teaspoon salt	

1. Bring the water and salt to a boil in a large kettle
2. Shuck the corn, cut off the ends and wash away any clinging silks.
3. Place the corn in the boiling water and when it returns to a boil, cover and turn off the heat.
4. When ready to eat, drain the corn and serve with butter, pepper, and more salt. It will hold in the covered kettle 20 minutes or thereabouts. Reheat if necessary.

FRESH CORN AND GREEN PEPPER

1 ear cooked corn (see recipe, above)	½ cup chopped green pepper
	Salt and pepper
1 tablespoon oil	1 tablespoon butter

1. Cut the kernels of cooked corn from the ear.
2. Heat the oil in a skillet and sauté the green pepper until tender, stirring to prevent burning.
3. Combine the corn and sautéed green pepper, salt and pepper and mix well.
4. Just before serving, heat the mixture and add the butter. Serve hot when the butter is melted.

CORN AND TOMATOES

1 ear corn	1 small onion, sliced
½ cup tomato sauce	Salt and pepper

1. Cut the corn kernels off the cob.
2. Place all ingredients in a saucepan and simmer covered 15 minutes. Serve hot.

CORN AND CELERY

1 ear corn	¼ teaspoon sugar
½ cup diced celery	½ teaspoon butter
Salt and pepper	

1. Cut the corn kernels off the cob.
2. Combine the corn, celery, salt, pepper and sugar and simmer 15 minutes or until the celery is almost tender.
3. Stir in the butter and serve hot.

CORN CASSEROLE

1 teaspoon butter	1 tablespoon chopped green
1 8½-ounce can creamed corn	pepper
1 tablespoon chopped onion	Salt and pepper
	2 crackers, crumbled

1. Melt the butter in a small casserole.
2. Add the creamed corn to the casserole and top with onion, green pepper, salt and pepper and cracker crumbs.
3. Place under the broiler at moderate heat and broil 20 minutes.

CORN CASSEROLE AND
TORTILLA CHIPS

1 tablespoon butter	2 tablespoons chopped green
1 8½-ounce can creamed corn	pepper
	¼ cup tortilla chips crushed

1. Butter bottom and sides of a small casserole.
2. Add the corn. Top with the green pepper and then the tortilla chips.
3. Place in a 350-degree oven for ½ hour or until bubbly. Serve hot.

Note: Salt and pepper may be added to your own taste.

CORN AND TOMATOES SAUTE

1 ear of cooked corn (see recipe, page 200)	1 small tomato, peeled, cored and diced (about ½ cup)
1 tablespoon butter	Salt and pepper

1. Slice the kernels of corn from the cob.
2. Melt the butter in a saucepan and sauté the tomato stirring for about 2 minutes.
3. Turn off the heat and stir in the cooked corn, salt and pepper.
4. When ready to serve, turn on the fire, stir again and serve hot.

EGGPLANT CASSEROLE

1 tablespoon vegetable oil	¼ teaspoon sugar
1 garlic clove, minced	1 8-ounce can (1 cup) stewed
½ cup chopped onion	tomatoes
¼ pound ground chuck steak	1 cup eggplant, cubed
Salt and pepper	3 shakes crushed red pepper

1. Heat the oil in a small casserole and sauté the garlic and onion for 2 minutes over medium heat.
2. Add the chopped meat to the casserole and then the salt, pepper and sugar. Stir to mix well and cook until the meat loses its red color.
3. Stir in the tomatoes and continue cooking for 2 minutes longer.
4. Finally add the cubed eggplant to the casserole, add red pepper, cover and simmer about ¾ hour or until the eggplant is tender and well blended. Check seasonings and serve hot.

EGGPLANT, QUICK AND GOOD

½ cup diced onion	1 cup diced eggplant
1 garlic clove, minced	1 8-ounce can stewed tomatoes
1 tablespoon olive or vegetable oil	Salt and pepper

1. Sauté the onion and garlic in the oil for 1 minute or until the onion is wilted. Do not burn.
2. Add the diced eggplant. Stir and cook another minute.
3. Pour the tomatoes over the eggplant, and add seasoning. Mix well and simmer covered for ½ hour. Serve hot.

EGGPLANT STEW

1 small eggplant or a 5-ounce piece	¼ cup canned tomatoes, seeded (use a sieve)
2 teaspoons oil	¼ teaspoon chopped parsley
1 tablespoon chopped onion	¼ teaspoon capers
1 garlic clove, minced	¼ teaspoon basil
2 tablespoons chopped green pepper	Salt and pepper

1. Wrap the eggplant in aluminum foil and bake 1 hour at 350 degrees.
2. Heat the oil and sauté the onion and garlic for 2 minutes stirring.
3. Add the green pepper and continue cooking another minute.
4. Add the tomatoes, parsley, capers, basil, salt and pepper and cook 5 minutes.
5. Unwrap the eggplant and scoop out the flesh and add it to the sauce. Discard the outside peel.
6. Mix well and reheat at serving time. Serve with lemon wedges if desired.

MOUSSAKA

4 slices eggplant, ¼-inch thick (about 5 ounces)
Flour for dredging
2 tablespoons olive oil
Salt and pepper
2 tablespoons butter plus enough to butter the casserole
1 garlic clove, minced
¼ cup chopped onion
¼ pound ground chuck steak

⅓ cup tomato sauce
1 bay leaf
¼ teaspoon oregano
¼ cup red wine
1 teaspoon chopped parsley
¼ cup chopped mushrooms
1 tablespoon flour
½ cup milk
1 egg yolk
Grated Parmesan cheese

1. Let the slices of eggplant stand in salted water for 20 minutes. Drain, rinse, and dry the slices.
2. Dredge the eggplant in seasoned flour and brown it in 1 tablespoon of the oil.
3. Heat 1 tablespoon of the butter in a skillet and sauté the garlic and onion until golden and add the ground meat. Stir and cook 10 minutes.
4. Add the tomato sauce, bay leaf, oregano, salt, pepper, wine and parsley and cook stirring frequently until the liquid is almost evaporated.
5. Cook the mushrooms in the remaining tablespoon of oil 3 minutes or until golden. Add them to the skillet.
6. Butter a small casserole or roasting pan and place 2 slices of eggplant on the bottom. Next layer in the meat sauce and then another layer of eggplant.
7. For bechamel sauce: Melt 1 tablespoon of butter and stir in 1 tablespoon of flour. Add the milk and stir with a wire whisk until slightly thickened. In a cup containing the egg yolk pour a little of the hot sauce. Blend well and add to the main body of sauce. Stir and heat but do not boil.
8. Pour the bechamel sauce over the casserole and sprinkle the Parmesan cheese on top. Bake at 400 degrees for 30 minutes. Let the casserole cool 10 minutes before serving.

EGGPLANT AND CHEESE CASSEROLE

½ cup peeled and diced eggplant	1 egg yolk
1 teaspoon vegetable oil	½ cup cracker crumbs
Salt and pepper	1 tablespoon tomato paste
½ cup grated cheese	2 tablespoons water

1. Sauté the eggplant in the oil in an ovenproof casserole for about 5 minutes stirring frequently.
2. Add the salt, pepper, cheese and egg yolk and mix well over low heat.
3. Top with cracker crumbs and pour over the tomato paste and water mixed well.
4. Bake 30 minutes at 350 degrees.

EGGPLANT WITH RICE AND CUMIN

2 teaspoons butter	2 tablespoons diced onion
3 ounces eggplant, diced (approximately ½ cup)	¼ cup canned tomatoes, sieved to remove the seeds
Salt and pepper	2 tablespoons rice
2 tablespoons diced green pepper	1 teaspoon cumin
	¼ cup chicken broth

1. Melt the butter in a small casserole and sauté the eggplant to tender but not mushy (about 15 minutes).
2. Season with salt and pepper.
3. Add all other ingredients and stir.
4. At or near serving time, bring to a boil and bake at 375 degrees for 20 minutes.
5. Stir again and serve hot.

Note: Top with grated Parmesan cheese if you desire.

BRAISED ENDIVE

1 endive	1 pinch salt
½ teaspoon lemon juice	2 tablespoons water
1 tablespoon butter	¼ teaspoon sugar

1. Trim ends and any outer, discolored leaves from the endive.
2. Place the endive in a small casserole with cover, add lemon juice, butter, salt, water, and sugar.
3. Cover, bring to a boil and cook over moderate heat 40 minutes or until tender.
4. Remove cover of casserole and brown the endive to a light caramel color in the pan juices. Add additional butter if required.

BRAISED ENDIVE AND BACON

1 endive, about ⅓ pound	Salt and pepper
1 strip bacon	

1. Trim the endive and peel off the outer leaves.
2. Wrap the bacon completely around the endive lengthwise. Tie with string.
3. Place the wrapped endive in a small casserole with tight fitting cover.
4. Salt and pepper the endive and cook covered on top of the stove over a flame tamer until the endive is tender (about 15 minutes).

WHITE ONION SPECIAL

4 small white onions	1 teaspoon heavy cream
1 teaspoon butter	Salt and pepper
1 teaspoon sugar	

1. Boil the onions in water to cover until tender. Drain.
2. Melt the butter in a small skillet and stir in the sugar. Add the onions and glaze in the hot sugar-butter sauce.
3. Turn off the heat and stir in the cream, season, and serve hot.

FRENCH PEAS

1 tablespoon butter
1 cup shredded lettuce

1 cup shelled peas (leave peas in shells until just before cooking)
Salt and pepper

1. Melt the butter in a saucepan with a tight fitting cover and add the lettuce, peas and seasonings.
2. Cover and cook very slowly over minimum heat for 1 hour or until the peas are tender.
3. Mix well and add a little more butter if you are not on a diet. Serve hot.

GREEN PEPPER STUFFED WITH FRESH CORN

1 ear corn
½ green pepper

Salt and pepper
1 tablespoon butter

1. Trim corn kernels off the cob.
2. Remove white membranes from the inside of the pepper.
3. Stuff pepper with corn kernels.
4. Top with salt, pepper, and butter.
5. Place in a small casserole, add a little water and cover. Simmer over a flame tamer until the pepper is tender (about 10 minutes).

POMME DE TERRE BUDAPEST

½ onion, minced
2 tablespoons butter
¼ teaspoon dry dill

¼ teaspoon paprika
1 cup sliced potatoes
   Salt and pepper
½ cup beef broth

1. Sauté the onion in the butter with dill and paprika.
2. Add the potatoes, salt and pepper and the broth.
3. Simmer under low flame until potatoes are done (about 15 minutes).
4. Reduce sauce and serve over potatoes.

HOT POTATO SALAD WITH BACON

3 small potatoes (about ¾ cup), cooked and sliced
3 strips bacon
1 tablespoon chopped onion
1 tablespoon vinegar

⅛ teaspoon dry mustard
1 teaspoon water
1 teaspoon sugar
½ teaspoon paprika
   Salt and pepper

1. Cook the potatoes in water to cover until they are tender. Cool, peel, and slice the potatoes and keep them warm in a casserole or suitable vessel with lid.
2. Fry the bacon until it is crisp. Break it into small pieces and distribute it over the potato slices.
3. Sauté the onion in 1 tablespoon of the bacon drippings until wilted.
4. Mix remaining ingredients and pour into the skillet with the onion. Bring to a boil and pour over the potatoes. Serve warm.

FRIED POTATOES THINLY SLICED

2 medium potatoes (about ¾ cup
   when sliced)

1 tablespoon butter
  Salt and pepper

1. Peel the potatoes and slice very thinly with a potato peeler.
2. Drop in cold water, drain, and dry with paper towels.
3. Melt the butter in a skillet, add the potatoes and cook over fairly high heat on one side pressing down with a spatula to encourage forming of a cake.
4. When set and browning around the edges, turn the cake and cook on the other side until done to the touch of a fork (about 15 minutes). Season with salt and pepper.

POTATO, EGG, AND CHEESE CASSEROLE

2 small cooked potatoes, sliced
1 hard boiled egg, sliced
  Salt and pepper
1 teaspoon butter

1 teaspoon flour
⅓ cup milk
2 tablespoons grated cheddar
  cheese

1. Place half the potatoes in the bottom of a small casserole. Top with egg slices and finish with the remaining potato slices.
2. Salt and pepper the casserole to taste.
3. Melt the butter in a saucepan and stir in the flour. Now pour in the milk all at once and stir until the mixture is smooth and beginning to thicken. Add the cheese and continue the stirring until the sauce is smooth again and well blended.
4. Pour the sauce over the casserole and place under the broiler until the top is well browned. Serve immediately.

SCALLOPED POTATOES

1 cup sliced potatoes	Salt and pepper
1 tablespoon butter	2 tablespoons grated cheddar
3 tablespoons cream	cheese
2 tablespoons flour	

1. Preheat the oven to 350 degrees.
2. Grease a small casserole with half the butter, add half the potatoes, 1 teaspoon of flour, and half the cream, the seasonings.
4. Repeat layers as above. Top with cheese and dot with butter.
5. Cover and cook ½ hour. Remove the cover for a few minutes toward the end of cooking time until the top of the dish is browned.

SCALLOPED POTATOES WITH GARLIC AND CHEESE

½ cup sliced potatoes	¼ teaspoon pepper
⅓ cup milk	1 teaspoon butter
½ garlic clove, minced	2 tablespoons grated cheese
¼ teaspoon salt	(cheddar or gruyère)

1. In a small pan place the potatoes, milk, garlic, salt and pepper and bring to a boil.
2. Butter a small baking dish and add the potato mixture.
3. Top with cheese and place in a 400 degree oven for 1 hour. Reduce the heat if the liquid is evaporating too quickly and the surface is too brown. I mean don't let it burn unless you like the flavor which isn't bad.

RATATOUILLE

1 tablespoon olive oil	¼ teaspoon parsley
½ cup chopped onion	¼ teaspoon thyme
1 garlic clove, minced	½ teaspoon basil
1 cup eggplant, in ½-inch cubes	1 cup fresh tomatoes, peeled, in
¼ cup green pepper, cored,	½-inch cubes
seeded, and coarsely chopped	Salt and freshly ground black
1 bay leaf	pepper

1. Heat the oil and sauté the onion and garlic for about 2 minutes. Stir to prevent burning or scorching.
2. Add the eggplant. Stir and cook another minute.
3. Add the green pepper, bay leaf, parsley, thyme and basil. Mix well.
4. Add the tomatoes, seasoning, and stir again.
5. Bake covered in a 350 degree oven for 20 minutes. Serve hot as a vegetable or cold as a first course.

Note: Any leftover ratatouille is good on the following day cold or warmed.

SPINACH

½ package spinach

1. Place spinach in water to cover in the sink or in a suitable bowl. Stir and wash thoroughly. Let stand in the water for several minutes at least.
2. Place the washed spinach in a heavy casserole with a tightly fitting lid. Turn the casserole over and drain all excess water from the spinach.
3. Place the covered casserole over the lowest heat until the spinach is thoroughly wilted. This should take no more than ½ hour.
4. Serve warm with white vinegar and sliced hard-cooked egg (optional).

TOMATO STUFFED WITH CORN

1 medium tomato	Salt and pepper
1 ear corn	½ tablespoon butter

1. Cut off the top of the tomato and scoop out the seeds and some of the pulp to make a tomato case for the corn.
2. Cook the corn according to the recipe (see page 200). Cool the ear of corn and cut off the kernels.
3. Chop the inside portion of the tomato which you have scooped out of the case and combine with the corn kernels. Salt and pepper the mixture.
4. Stuff the tomato with the above preparation. Top with the butter and place under the broiler for a few minutes or until the tomato is softened.

Note: A little minced green pepper is very good as an addition to this recipe or as alternative or variation.

ZUCCHINI, POTATOES, AND TOMATOES

1 small zucchini, in ¼-inch slices	1 small potato, diced
1 tablespoon olive oil	¼ teaspoon oregano
¼ cup slices onion	Salt and pepper
¼ cup stewed tomatoes or minced fresh tomatoes	Freshly grated Parmesan cheese (optional)

1. Sauté the zucchini in oil over high heat for about 3 minutes, stirring constantly to prevent burning. It should be a golden color.
2. Add the other ingredients except cheese, cover and simmer until the potatoes are done. Test them with a fork.
3. Serve hot with a cheese garnish to your taste (optional).

ZUCCHINI AND VEGETABLE CASSEROLE

1 tablespoon olive oil
1 garlic clove, minced
1 small zucchini, sliced
1 small tomato, peeled and sliced
¼ cup minced onion

¼ cup diced green pepper
1 rib celery, trimmed and diced
Salt and pepper
3 tablespoons grated Parmesan cheese

1. Pour the oil into a small casserole and sprinkle the minced garlic over it.
2. Add layers of zucchini, tomato, onion, green pepper and celery. Sprinkle with salt and pepper.
3. Cover and bake at 300 degrees for ½ hour.
4. Uncover, add the cheese and return to the oven for another ½ hour.

ZUCCHINI CHEESE CASSEROLE

2 tablespoons butter or margarine
1 garlic clove, minced
1 small onion, sliced
1 medium zucchini

Salt and pepper
¼ teaspoon oregano
4 ounces stewed tomatoes
½ cup grated cheddar cheese

1. Melt margarine or butter in a small casserole and sauté garlic and onion for 3 minutes.
2. Add thinly sliced zucchini, salt, pepper and oregano and cook covered for 10 minutes.
3. Add tomatoes and place in a 400 degree oven for 15 minutes.
4. Uncover and add the cheese; return to the oven until the cheese is melted. Serve immediately.

ZUCCHINI WITH TOMATOES

1 zucchini (about ½ pound)
¼ pound red ripe tomatoes
1½ teaspoons olive oil
2 tablespoons finely chopped onion

½ teaspoon finely minced garlic
¼ teaspoon dried basil
Salt and pepper

1. Trim ends of the zucchini and cut into 1-inch slices.
2. Peel the tomatoes, seed them and cut in small cubes.
3. Heat the oil in a small casserole and sauté the onions to translucent stirring to prevent browning.
4. Add the garlic, tomatoes, basil, salt and pepper. Stir again and cook about 5 minutes over low heat.
5. Now add the zucchini, cover and cook 20 minutes. Stir occasionally. The zucchini should be tender but crisp.

ZUCCHINI PROVENCALE

1 teaspoon bacon fat or butter
1 small onion, thinly sliced
½ garlic clove, minced finely
¼ cup green pepper, diced
Salt and freshly ground black pepper

¼ teaspoon basil
¼ teaspoon oregano
2 teaspoons tomato paste
½ cup canned tomatoes
1 small zucchini, sliced

1. In the heated bacon fat or butter sauté the onion and garlic to golden. Do not burn.
2. Add the green pepper and stir. Cook 1 minute and add salt and pepper. Then add the basil and oregano.
3. Stir in the tomatoes and tomato paste.
4. Now add the sliced zucchini, mix well, cover and simmer over low heat 1 hour. Serve hot.

SMOTHERED FRESH VEGETABLES

1 small zucchini	1 ear corn
1 small tomato	1 tablespoon oil
1 small potato	Salt and pepper
1 small onion	

1. Slice the vegetables, about ½ cup of each, except the corn very thin.
2. Cook the corn according to the recipe (page 200) or use a left-over ear from yesterday. Trim the kernels from the ear.
3. Heat the oil in a small skillet and coat the entire bottom and sides by rolling the skillet and tilting it. Turn off the heat.
4. Arrange the sliced vegetables in the skillet: zucchini, onion, potato and tomato in that order and sprinkle the corn kernels on top. Salt and pepper each layer lightly.
5. Cover the skillet with a sheet of aluminum foil, place over a flame tamer and low heat and cook ¾ hour or until the vegetables are all tender.

Note: Butter may be added to the top of the dish before covering and this is recommended if you can take the calories. Also the vegetables may be varied. To provide a complete lunch or light dinner break an egg on top of the hot vegetables and cook until it sets.

SHERRY KRAUT

1 pound sauerkraut	Freshly ground black pepper
1 onion sliced	Sherry
1 garlic clove, minced	

1. Place kraut, onion, garlic and pepper in a heavy casserole and add sherry just to cover.
2. Simmer 2 hours or until ready to serve.

Note: Serve with browned pork chop or frankfurters added to the pot for the final cooking and boiled new potatoes. For one meal, use one large, drained spoonful of sauerkraut, one pork chop, and two small new potatoes. It's good and wait until you weigh. (I did it 2 days in succession and lost 3 pounds). Use any leftover sherry kraut as a luncheon soup.

Miscellaneous

Corn Bread • Hot Water Corn Bread
Cornmeal Crêpes • Corn Fritters
Pancakes • Pastry Crust • Two Biscuits
Chiffonade Dressing • French Dressing
Russian Dressing • Roquefort Dressing
Thousand Island Dressing—1 • Thousand Island Dressing—2
Cheese Sauce • Creole Sauce • Curry Sauce
Hollandaise Sauce • Mayonnaise • Sauce Aurore
Tomato Sauce • Quick Tomato Sauce
Marinara • Meat Sauce for Spaghetti
Brownies • Five-Flavor Fudge
Maple Syrup-Pecan Fudge • Rice Pudding • Flan for One
Flan with Lime Flavor • Indian Pudding

In the miscellaneous category I have included sauces and dressings (the largest group), corn bread, pancakes, pastry crust, biscuits, crêpes and fritters, and finally desserts: brownies, rice pudding, flan, Indian pudding and my two favorite fudge recipes. I use these recipes as much or more than any in the other sections.

CORN BREAD

¼ cup cornmeal
1 teaspoon flour
¼ teaspoon sugar
1 teaspoon baking powder

⅛ teaspoon salt
1 egg
¼ cup milk
1 tablespoon butter, melted

1. Sift dry ingredients into a mixing bowl.
2. Add the egg, milk, and butter and beat until well mixed and smooth.
3. Bake in buttered muffin cups or pyrex muffin molds for 25 minutes at 400 degrees.

   Note: For one muffin, do the following:

2 tablespoons cornmeal
1 teaspoon flour
1 teaspoon baking powder
¼ teaspoon sugar

⅛ teaspoon salt
1 egg yolk
2 tablespoons milk
1 tablespoon butter, melted

Follow directions above. It's a smaller portion, but enough for 1 and it is better.

HOT WATER CORN BREAD

1 teaspoon butter
¼ cup cornmeal
1 teaspoon flour
½ teaspoon baking powder

A pinch of salt
1 teaspoon sugar
¼ cup plus 1 tablespoon boiling water

1. Place ample butter in two muffin cups (about ½ teaspoon in each or as rich as you like it). Place the cups over the pilot light so that the butter melts. Then rotate and tip the cups to coat all sides of each cup.
2. Mix all ingredients well and pour half into each cup.

3. Bake at 400 degrees for 25 minutes.

Note: The above makes one nice sized muffin; however using two cups and ample butter allows more delicious crust to form. I recommend this procedure, but choose your favorite texture.

CORNMEAL CREPES

1 tablespoon flour	2 tablespoons milk
2 teaspoons cornmeal	Salt
1 egg yolk	1 teaspoon butter, melted

1. Place flour and meal in a bowl.
2. Beat the yolk and milk and stir it into the dry mixture.
3. Add the salt and melted butter and mix well.
4. Spoon into greased crêpe pan or skillet and cook to brown on both sides. Serve hot.

CORN FRITTERS

⅓ cup cream-style corn	1 tablespoon milk
1 egg, separated	1 teaspoon vegetable oil or
1 tablespoon flour	enough to grease the skillet
1 tablespoon cornmeal	
Salt and pepper	

1. Place the corn in a small bowl and add the egg yolk, flour, meal, salt, and pepper. Stir well and mix in the milk.
2. Beat the egg white stiff and fold it in.
3. Oil a small skillet or griddle and spoon in the batter in desired quantities.
4. Brown on both sides over medium low heat. It makes about seven small, tablespoon sized cakes.

PANCAKES

2 tablespoons flour	1 egg
¼ teaspoon salt	¼ cup milk
¼ teaspoon sugar	1 teaspoon butter

1. Sift flour, salt, and sugar onto a sheet of wax paper.
2. Empty the sifted ingredients into a glass jar with a tight fitting top. (Alternatively use a small bowl and spoon).
3. Add the egg and milk to the dry ingredients in the jar and shake well with the top on securely. Stir around the bottom edges of the jar to dislodge any clinging flour, replace the top and shake again.
4. Grease lightly a griddle or frying pan. Pour about a quarter of the batter onto the griddle to make each pancake. Brown the pancakes on both sides.

Note: A cured pan is best for cooking the pancakes. If you don't have one, make one by heating oil very hot in a new pan and letting it stand overnight. Then, never wash the pan with soap and water after using. Use salt and paper towels to clean the cured pan.

PASTRY CRUST

¼ cup flour	2 teaspoons lard
⅛ teaspoon salt	1 tablespoon ice water

1. Place the flour and salt in a mixing bowl and cut in the lard. Use a small bowl just large enough for one hand to work the flour, salt, and lard. This will take some time and needs to be done carefully and thoroughly. Make sure that all lard is worked into the flour and that no lumps remain. The end result should appear rather grainy.

2. Add the water and continue working the dough until it can be gathered into a ball. Knead the dough well in the hands. Refrigerate the kneaded dough for at least ½ hour.
3. Flour a bread board or put wax paper on your counter and flour it. Also flour a rolling pin and roll out the dough to rather thin.
4. Use this dough as topping for a meat pie and bake at 400 degrees for ½ hour. Brown by placing under the broiler for a few minutes.

Note: A tin can with top and bottom removed makes a good biscuit cutter and can be used as a rolling pin for a small quantity of dough such as this recipe produces.

TWO BISCUITS

¼ cup flour
⅛ teaspoon salt
1 teaspoon baking powder

1 teaspoon shortening
2 tablespoons milk

1. Sift the flour, salt and baking powder into a bowl and cut in the shortening with a pastry cutter, a salad fork, or by hand. Stir, cut, and blend well until the mixture appears grainy.
2. Add the milk and continue mixing until you can form a ball of dough. Knead the ball well and pack it tightly.
3. On a floured sheet of wax paper and using a floured rolling pin or the palm of your hand roll out the dough and cut into rounds using a biscuit cutter or a small can open at both ends. (The small can may also be used as a rolling pin).
4. Reroll the scraps and fashion another biscuit with the cutter or by hand.
5. Bake on a sheet of aluminum foil at 450 degrees for 12 minutes.

CHIFFONADE DRESSING

1 tablespoon vegetable or olive
   oil
½ tablespoon vinegar
   Salt and pepper
1 hard-cooked egg, chopped

1 teaspoon chopped green
   pepper
1 teaspoon chopped parsley
1 teaspoon chopped onion

Mix all ingredients and refrigerate prior to serving.

FRENCH DRESSING

1 teaspoon wine vinegar
   Salt and freshly ground pepper

1 tablespoon olive oil

Place the vinegar and seasoning in a salad bowl and add the oil slowly beating with a wire whisk.

Note: The above is recommended; however substitutions are possible. Other vinegars and other oils are also good and combinations may also be made. And don't overlook the variations on this base possible by the addition of mustard, cheese, capers, tomato and many other tastes.

Always make fresh dressing just before tossing the greens. One hint: place all ingredients in a small jar with tight fitting cover and shake well to mix.

RUSSIAN DRESSING

2 tablespoons mayonnaise
1 tablespoon ketchup or chili sauce

2 teaspoons India relish or pepper relish

Mix all ingredients well and serve cold over greens.

ROQUEFORT DRESSING

1 tablespoon roquefort cheese
1½ tablespoons olive oil

¼ teaspoon lemon juice

Break up the cheese with a fork and shake with other ingredients in a jar with the top on tight until well blended. Remove the top and make sure there is no cheese sticking to the sides of the jar. If there is, scrape it into the blend, retop the jar and give it another final shake.

This dressing may be made in advance and given its last shake just after removal from the refrigerator and before serving.

THOUSAND ISLAND DRESSING—1

2 tablespoons mayonnaise
1 teaspoon chili sauce
1 teaspoon minced stuffed olives
1 teaspoon chopped green pepper

1 teaspoon minced scallions or chives
1 tablespoon cream

Mix all ingredients well and chill before serving.

THOUSAND ISLAND DRESSING—2

2 tablespoons mayonnaise	1 tablespoon minced onion
1 teaspoon chili sauce	1 teaspoon sweet pepper relish
Salt and pepper	1 tablespoon cream

Mix all ingredients well and serve cold over the salad greens.

CHEESE SAUCE

1 tablespoon butter	⅔ cup grated cheddar cheese
1 tablespoon flour	Salt
½ cup milk	½ teaspoon worcestershire sauce

1. In a small saucepan, blend flour and butter over low heat and cook 1 minute.
2. Add the milk stirring rapidly with a wire whisk until the sauce is smooth and thickened.
3. Add the cheese, salt and worcestershire sauce and blend well. The sauce is finished when the cheese is melted and thorouhgly incorporated. It may be made a little in advance and reheated at serving time.

Note: This sauce is good over cauliflower, broccoli, or other vegetables as well as over poached eggs, etc.

CREOLE SAUCE

1 tablespoon oil	¼ teaspoon rosemary
½ cup chopped shallots or onion	1 bay leaf
1 garlic clove, minced	¼ teaspoon thyme
½ cup chopped green pepper	3 drops worcestershire sauce
1 8-ounce can (or 1 cup) of Italian plum tomatoes	1 slice lemon
	Salt and pepper

1. Heat the oil in a saucepan and saute the onion, garlic and green pepper for several minutes stirring constantly.
2. Sieve the tomatoes into the saucepan and discard the tomato seeds. Add remaining ingredients. Stir well and simmer for ½ hour or so until all ingredients are cooked to your taste. They may be soft or slightly resistant to the bite.

Note: Serve the creole sauce with cooked shrimp, in an omelet, or as a sauce with meat loaf, veal, etc.

CURRY SAUCE

1 tablespoon butter
1 garlic clove, finely chopped or passed through a garlic press
1 tablespoon onion, finely chopped
1 tablespoon apple, finely chopped
1 tablespoon banana, finely chopped

½ tablespoon tomato sauce
⅓ cup chicken broth
1 tablespoon curry powder
Salt and pepper
1 teaspoon each of butter and flour mixed well to for a paste for thickening
2 tablespoons cream

1. Melt the butter in a suitable saucepan or small casserole and sauté the garlic for a second or so. Add the onion, stir and then add the apple and finally the banana. Keep stirring over low heat and blend well.
2. Add the tomato sauce, chicken broth, curry powder, salt and pepper and continue blending and cooking slowly for 2 minutes.
3. Add the thickening paste gradually and blend well.
4. Add the cream and mix well and keep warm until serving time.

Note: Use this sauce with shrimp, chicken, turkey, or whatever you fancy in a curry sauce. It may be varied slightly in ingredients to your particular taste. In other words: thicker or thinner or hotter by the addition of pepper.

HOLLANDAISE SAUCE

3 tablespoons butter
1 egg yolk
1 tablespoon cold water

1 teaspoon lemon juice
1 pinch salt or to taste
1 shake cayenne

1. Simmer ½-inch water in a skillet.
2. Melt the butter in a saucepan or other suitable container. Reserve the melted butter.
3. Place a saucepan a little smaller than the skillet into the skillet of simmering water.
4. Add the egg yolk and water and beat with a wire whisk for a minute or so until the egg becomes light in color.
5. Remove the pan from the skillet and add the butter a little at a time beating well. Continue for a few minutes until the sauce becomes thicker. Return to the simmering water in the skillet if necessary to aid the thickening.
6. Season the sauce with the lemon, salt, and pepper and continue the beating.
7. Set the sauce aside and when serving time arrives return to the simmering water and give a liberal number of beats and test for seasonings. You may desire more salt or lemon.

MAYONNAISE

1 egg yolk
Salt and freshly ground black pepper
¼ teaspoon dry mustard

2 teaspoons lemon juice
⅛ teaspoon cayenne
¾ cup olive oil
2 teaspoons water

1. Place the egg yolk in a bowl and add the seasonings.
2. With a wire whisk or an electric beater, start beating.
3. Add the oil a drop or so at a time until all the oil is incorporated.
4. Now beat in the water, place the mayonnaise in a jar and refrigerate. You will have almost a cup and it will keep several weeks.

SAUCE AURORE

1⅓ teaspoons butter
1 teaspoon chopped onion
¼ garlic clove, minced
1 tablespoon tomato paste
⅛ teaspoon thyme
⅛ bay leaf

Salt and pepper
½ teaspoon flour
2 tablespoons chicken broth
1 tablespoon heavy cream
1 teaspoon port wine

1. Melt half the butter and wilt the onion and garlic in it.
2. Add the tomato paste, thyme, bay leaf, salt and pepper and bring to a boil. Simmer 15 minutes or so.
3. In the meantime, melt the remaining butter, stir in the flour, and gradually stir in the chicken broth.
4. When the sauce begins to thicken add the tomato sauce, and simmer about ½ hour.
5. To finish add the cream and port. Stir well and keep warm to serving time.

Note: Serve the sauce over poached chicken, hard-boiled eggs, fish or use your imagination.

TOMATO SAUCE

1 teaspoon olive oil
1 garlic clove, finely chopped
1 onion minced

1 8-ounce can Italian plum tomatoes, sieved
¼ teaspoon each thyme and basil
Salt and freshly ground pepper

1. Heat the oil in a saucepan and sauté the garlic and onion for a minute or two until the onion becomes translucent and the scent of garlic is in the air.
2. Add the tomatoes and other ingredients and simmer for ½ hour.

QUICK TOMATO SAUCE

1 tablespoon butter	½ teaspoon dried basil,
½ teaspoon garlic, finely chopped	pulverized in a mortar and
1 cup canned tomatoes, strained	pestle
	Salt and pepper

1. Melt the butter and add the garlic. Stir and cook 1 minute.
2. Add the tomatoes, basil, salt, and pepper. Mix well and simmer 20 minutes.

Note: This sauce is good over spaghetti with a topping of freshly grated Parmesan cheese.

MARINARA SAUCE FOR SPAGHETTI

1 tablespoon olive oil	1 8-ounce can Italian plum
1 small onion, minced (about ¼ cup)	tomatoes
	Salt and pepper
1 garlic clove, finely minced	1 tablespoon butter
1 small carrot, minced	¼ teaspoon oregano
	¼ teaspoon dried basil

1. Heat the oil in a skillet and cook the onion, garlic and carrot to a golden brown stirring constantly to prevent burning.
2. Sieve the tomatoes to remove the seeds. Add the tomatoes to the skillet.
3. Add salt and pepper to taste and simmer the sauce about 15 minutes.
4. Pass all through a sieve or food mill and return to the skillet with the remaining ingredients. Simmer partially covered ½ hour.

MEAT SAUCE FOR SPAGHETTI

1 tablespoon olive oil	¼ teaspoon basil
4 ounces ground chuck steak	1 clove
1 teaspoon salt	8 ounces Italian plum tomatoes
1 garlic clove, minced	3 tablespoons tomato paste
1 onion, finely chopped	1 bay leaf
¼ teaspoon peppercorns, crushed	1 tablespoon butter
2 tablespoons white wine or vermouth	

1. Heat the oil in a small skillet or casserole and add the ground chuck, salt and pepper. Stir until the meat begins to lose its reddish color.
2. Add the garlic and onion and continue stirring until the meat is thoroughly browned.
3. Add the peppercorns, wine or vermouth, basil, and clove and cook stirring until the wine evaporates.
4. Add the tomatoes pressed through a sieve to separate the seeds. Discard the seeds. Add the tomato paste, bay leaf and butter. Simmer partially covered for 2 or 3 hours.

Note: This sauce may be served over about 3-ounces of spaghetti cooked 10 minutes in boiling salted water and drained. This is a heavily sauced dish but good. If not to your taste, use half the sauce for a portion of spaghetti and retain the remainder for another day. (It improves with a day or so of age.)

BROWNIES

2 squares unsweetened chocolate	1 cup sugar
¼ cup butter	½ cup flour
½ teaspoon vanilla	½ teaspoon baking powder
2 eggs	½ teaspoon salt

1. Preheat oven to 350 degrees.
2. Melt chocolate and butter in top of a double boiler (alternately use a saucepan placed in 1 inch simmering water in a skillet). Stir in vanilla.
3. Beat eggs lightly and gradually beat in sugar, chocolate mixture and then sift in flour, baking powder and salt.
4. Pour mixture into a greased pan and bake 25 minutes. Let cool and cut into squares.
5. Wrap in waxed paper in threes (ample servings for one) and freeze. Don't eat all at once.

FIVE FLAVOR FUDGE

2 squares unsweetened chocolate	1 cup milk
2 cups sugar	2 tablespoons butter
1 tablespoon light corn syrup	1 teaspoon vanilla extract
1 teaspoon salt	1 teaspoon almond extract

1. Melt chocolate, add sugar, corn syrup, salt, and milk. Cook over low heat stirring only until the sugar is dissolved.
2. Continue cooking until the syrup forms a soft ball in cold water.
3. Remove from heat and add the butter, and vanilla and almond extracts.
4. When the syrup has become quite cool, beat in as much air as possible and pour it into a buttered dish. Cut into squares before the fudge has completely hardened.

MAPLE SYRUP-PECAN FUDGE

2 cups maple syrup	¼ cup milk
1 tablespoon light corn syrup	1 teaspoon vanilla
½ cup heavy cream	1 cup chopped pecans

1. Combine syrups, cream, and milk in a saucepan.
2. Stir mixture over moderate heat until it begins to boil; continue cooking without stirring until a few drops form a soft ball in cold water.
3. Remove pan from heat and let cool to lukewarm.
4. Beat until the syrup begins to thicken.
5. Add vanilla and nuts, mix and pour into a buttered dish.
6. Cut into squares before fudge has completely hardened.
   Yield: About 30 one-inch squares. (Don't eat it all at once. It will refrigerate.)

RICE PUDDING

¾ cup water	¼ teaspoon vanilla
Salt	1 egg
¼ cup rice	1½ ounces raisins
¼ cup milk	⅛ teaspoon grated lemon rind
4 teaspoons sugar	1 teaspoon butter

1. Bring salted water to a boil and add the rice, stir and cover. Turn the heat to lowest and cook until the water is almost evaporated (about 20 minutes).
2. Drain and rinse the rice.
3. Mix well milk, salt, sugar, vanilla, egg, raisins, and lemon rind.
4. Add the rice to the mixture and mix well again. Pour into a small buttered baking dish.
5. Bake in a moderate oven (about 350 degrees) for about 30 minutes or until set.
6. Serve cold or hot with cream or ice cream.

FLAN FOR ONE

2½ tablespoons sugar
4 tablespoons cream
1 egg yolk

½ teaspoon almond or vanilla extract

1. Melt 2 tablespoons of the sugar in a small skillet. Stir well and let it form a caramel sauce.
2. Into a heated ovenproof custard cup, pour the caramel and turn and tip the cup to coat the bottom and sides of the cup. Set aside.
3. Place the cream in another custard cup and in turn place this in a larger vessel like a small skillet; fill the skillet with hot water to about 1 inch.
4. Let the low heat bring the cream to a low simmer. Watch closely for just beginning bubbles around the sides of the cream.
5. Place the egg yolk in another ovenproof cup. Break the yolk and stir.
6. When the bubbles appear in the cream, remove it from the flame and add the remaining sugar and the flavoring.
7. Now pour the cream very slowly into the egg mixture and stir well.
8. Lastly pour the egg-cream mixture into the caramel coated container. Place this in a larger vessel filled with hot water to 1 inch. Place this in the oven and bake at 350 degrees for 1 hour or until a knife inserted in the center of the custard comes out clean.
9. Refrigerate and serve at your leisure.

FLAN WITH LIME FLAVOR

3 tablespoons sugar
1 teaspoon lime juice
¼ teaspoon grated lime rind

¼ cup light cream
2 egg yolks

1. In a small heavy skillet place 2 tablespoons of the sugar. Stir occasionally over medium heat until the sugar begins to melt. Then stir continuously until it is a light brown. Pour immediately into a warm ovenproof custard cup or a similar ovenproof container. (You can warm the vessel over the pilot light on top of the stove in a few minutes). Tilt the cup and coat all sides with the caramel as high as possible.
2. Combine the grated lime rind and the lime juice.
3. Add the cream to another custard cup which has been placed in a small skillet of warm water. Place over low heat.
4. Add the yolks to a small bowl and mix lightly.
5. When the cream begins to simmer and form a light skin on top, remove it from the heat and stir in the remaining sugar.
6. Add the cream a little at a time to the yolks stirring constantly. Stir in the lime mixture and pour into the caramel-coated cup. Place in a 350 degree oven for 1 hour or until a knife inserted in the center of the custard comes out clean.
7. Refrigerate after the custard cools to room temperature. One hour or so will do or you can let the flan remain in the refrigerator overnight or longer.
8. At serving time, run a knife around the cup and invert to let the flan mold onto a serving plate. Serve alone or with fruit, fresh or preserved.

INDIAN PUDDING

½ cup milk	A pinch of cinnamon
2 teaspoons yellow cornmeal	Salt
4 teaspoons dark molasses	½ teaspoon butter
4 teaspoons sugar	

1. Place the milk in a saucepan over low heat and bring to a boil. Gradually add the cornmeal stirring with a wire whisk.
2. Now add the molasses and keep stirring.

3. Add the sugar, cinnamon and salt and stir well.
4. Butter a muffin cup or other suitable ovenproof container and add the mixture.
5. Bake 1 hour at 300 degrees. Serve with ice cream, whipped cream, or plain cream.

Index